THE WINTER PASCHA
Readings for the Christmas-Epiphany Season

THOMAS HOPKO

THE WINTER PASCHA
Readings for the Christmas-Epiphany Season

ST VLADIMIR'S SEMINARY PRESS
CRESTWOOD, NEW YORK 10707

Library of Congress Cataloging-in-Publication Data

Hopko, Thomas.
    The Winter Pascha.

1. Advent—Prayer-books and devotions—English.
2. Christmas—Prayer-books and devotions—English.
3. Epiphany season—Prayer-books and devotions—English.
4. Orthodox Eastern Church—Prayer-books and devotions—English.
I. Title.

BX383.H663   1984   242'.33 84-27622
ISBN 0-88141-025-X

THE WINTER PASCHA

Copyright © 1984

ST VLADIMIR'S SEMINARY PRESS

575 Scarsdale Road, Crestwood, NY 10707
www.svspress.com • 1-800-204-2665

ISBN 978-0-88141-025-9

PRINTED IN THE UNITED STATES OF AMERICA

† In grateful memory of Fr ALEXANDER SCHMEMANN who, with so many wonderful things, gave us also the title of this book.

Contents

1

The Winter Pascha

When winter begins to make its way into the northern hemisphere, the Church of Christ begins to celebrate a "splendid three-day Pascha." These words of the Typikon of the Orthodox Church, the instructions for liturgical worship, are explained by modern Russian Orthodox commentators in this way:

The feast of the Nativity of Christ belongs to the number of the twelve major feasts of the Church. Yet none of these feasts is celebrated by the Church with as much solemnity as the festival of Christ's Nativity. It is called *Pascha*: a splendid three-day Pascha.[1]

In old editions of the *Typikon,* similarly to the feast of Christ's Glorious Resurrection, the feast of Christ's Nativity is called *Pascha.* This emphasizes its close connection with the mystery of our salvation and deliverance from sin and death; the mystery which the holy Church proclaims in her dogmatic teachings and with which she brings us into direct spiritual contact in her liturgical services and sacraments.[2]

[1]K. Nikol'skii *Posobiye k Izucheniyu Ustava Bogosluzheniya Phavoslavnoi Tserkvi* (Guide to the understanding of the liturgical Typikon of the Orthodox Church), St. Petersburgh, 1900, p. 539. The festival of Christ's Resurrection, the original Pascha, is not one of the twelve major feasts of the Orthodox Church. In the Orthodox Tradition the feast of Christ's Resurrection stands alone, being, as the eighth ode of the paschal canon says, "the feast of feasts, holy day of holy days."

[2]*Nastol'naya Kniga Sviashchenosluzhitelia* (Handbook for the liturgical minister), Moscow Patriarchate, Moscow, 1977, p. 511.

The liturgical services for Christmas, officially called The Nativity According to the Flesh of Our Lord and God and Savior Jesus Christ, are consciously patterned after the services for the festival of the Pascha of the Lord, the holy Resurrection. There is a forty-day fast. There are prefeast preparations. There are the special royal hours with their prophecies, epistles, gospels, and hymns on the eve of the feast, followed by the vesperal liturgy of St Basil the Great. There is the solemn all-night vigil, crowned by the matin's canon and hymns. And finally, after the eucharistic celebration of St John Chrysostom on the day of the feast itself, the celebration continues to its completion in the festival of The Meeting of the Lord in the Temple forty days later. At the center of the festal season remains the original "Festival of Lights," the holy Epiphany, officially called in the Orthodox Church The Holy Theophany of Our Lord and God and Savior Jesus Christ.

The liturgical verses and hymns for Christmas and Epiphany, the Pascha of Christ's incarnation and manifestation in the flesh, repeat those of Easter, the Pascha of Christ's death and resurrection. The Lord's birth and baptism are directly connected to His dying and rising. He was born in order to die. He was baptized in order to be raised. The con-holy Epiphany, officially called in the Orthodox Church, The harmony between the events is overwhelming. The beauty of it is almost more than the believer can bear.

Today He who hung the earth upon the waters
is hung upon the tree.
> Today He who holds the whole creation in His hand
> is born of a virgin.
The King of angels is decked with a crown of thorns.
> He whose essence none can touch is bound
> in swaddling-clothes as a mortal man.
He who wraps the heavens in a cloud
is wrapped in the purple of mockery.
> God who in the beginning fashioned the heavens
> lies in a manger.
He who freed Adam in the Jordan

is slapped in the face.
He who rained manna on His people in the wilderness
is fed on milk from His mother's breast.
The Bridegroom of the Church is affixed
to the cross with nails.
The Bridegroom of the Church summons the wise men.
The Son of the Virgin is pierced with a spear.
The Son the Virgin accepts their gifts.
We worship Thy Passion, O Christ!
We worship Thy Passion, O Christ!
We worship Thy Passion, O Christ!
We worship Thy Nativity, O Christ!
We worship Thy Nativity, O Christ!
We worship Thy Nativity, O Christ!
Show us also Thy glorious Resurrection!
Show us also Thy glorious Theophany![3]

Jesus lay as an infant in the cavern in the reign of Caesar
Augustus that He might lay in the tomb under Pontius Pilate.
He was hounded by Herod that He might be caught by
Caiaphas. He was buried in baptism that He might descend
into death through the Cross. He was worshipped by wise
men that the whole of creation might adore Him in His
triumph over death. The Pascha of His Cross was prepared
by the Pascha of His Coming. The Pascha of His Resurrection was begun by the Pascha of His Incarnation. The Pascha
of His Glorification was foretold by the Pascha of His Baptism. This is what Christians celebrate each year in what
Father Alexander Schmemann was the first to call "the
Winter Pascha."[4]

---

[3]Verses sung at the service of matins and the ninth hour on Great and
Holy Friday and on Christmas Eve.

[4]While the Typikon of the Orthodox Church calls Christmas "a splendid
three-day Pascha," the expression "Winter Pascha" was coined by Father
Alexander Schmemann, late Dean and Professor of Liturgical Theology at
St Vladimir's Seminary, to whose memory this book is dedicated.

2

Come and See

The Christmas-Epiphany season in the Orthodox Church begins with a forty-day fasting period which starts on the feast of "the holy and all-praised apostle Philip." For this reason Christmas lent is sometimes called "the fast of Philip."[1] Although the coincidence of the feast of the apostle Philip and the beginning of the Christmas fast is accidental, humanly speaking, the eyes of faith may see in it a certain providence of God.

According to St John's gospel, Philip is one of the first of the apostles to be called by Jesus. On the day after the calling of Andrew and another of St John the Baptist's disciples, who, since he is not named, is probably the apostle John himself, Philip is called by the Lord. Like Andrew who went and called his brother Simon Peter, Philip goes and calls his friend Nathanael. The story is told in the gospel in this way:

> The next day Jesus decided to go to Galilee. And He found Philip and said to him, "Follow me." Now Philip was from Bethsaida, the city of Andrew and Peter. Philip found Nathanael, and said to him, "We have found Him of whom Moses in the law and also the prophets wrote, Jesus of Nazareth, the son of Joseph." Nathanael said to him, "Can anything good come out of Nazareth?" Philip said to him, "Come

[1]The feast of the apostle Philip is celebrated on November 14. The Orthodox Church does not traditionally use the term Advent for the Christmas fast. The word, however, is a perfectly good one, belonging to the common tradition of the Church in the West. It simply means "Coming."

and see." Jesus saw Nathanael coming to Him, and said of him, "Behold, an Israelite indeed, in whom is no guile!" Nathanael said to Him, "How do You know me?" Jesus answered him, "Before Philip called you, when you were under the fig tree, I saw you." Nathanael answered Him, "Rabbi, You are the Son of God! You are the King of Israel!" Jesus answered him, "Because I said to you, I saw you under the fig tree, do you believe? You shall see greater things than these." And He said to him, "Truly, truly, I say to you, you will see heaven opened, and the angels of God ascending and descending upon the Son of man." (Jn 1:43-51)

The story is typical of St John's gospel. The people first encounter the man "Jesus of Nazareth, the son of Joseph." They meet Him as a man, the one "of whom Moses in the law and also the prophets wrote." Then they go further. What they come to see is that this man is not merely the promised prophet and teacher; He is the Anointed, the Christ, the Messiah, the King of Israel. He is the Son of God. Indeed, He is God Himself in human form.

The pattern in St John's gospel is always the same. We see it in the narratives of the paralytic at the pool, the Samaritan woman at the well, the boy born blind, the encounter of Martha and Mary with Jesus at the tomb of Lazarus. The sequence of events is identical. It is a necessary sequence, not only *historically,* but *spiritually* and *mystically.*

We must first come to see Jesus the man. We must come to know Him as a concrete human being, a Jew, a rabbi, a prophet. We must meet Him as Mary's child, the carpenter's son, the Nazarene. Then, in this encounter, when our eyes are open and our hearts are pure, we can come to see "greater things." We can come to know Him not simply as a teacher, but the Teacher; not simply as a prophet, but the Prophet. We can come to know Him not merely as a son of man, but as the Son of man foretold by the prophet Daniel.[2] We can

2See Dan 7:13-14.

come to see Him not simply as a son of God, but as the Son of God, begotten of the Father before all ages.[3] We can come to recognize Him as God's Word in human flesh, as God's Image in human form.[4] And finally, we can come to see Him as God Himself; not the Father but the Father's Son, divine with the Father's own divinity, sent into the world for its salvation.[5]

The first step on the way of the Winter Pascha is the encounter with the man Jesus. We are invited with Philip and the disciples, to "come and see." If we want to come and want to see, we will. Like the first disciples, we will see "greater things" than we ever expected. We will see "heaven opened and the angels of God ascending and descending upon the Son of man." We will see Jesus as our Master, and will cry to Him: "Rabbi, You are the Son of God! You are the King of Israel!" And we will come to know Him for who and what He really is. But first we must come. For if we do not come, we will never see.

O God-seer Philip,
With divine inspiration and instruction of the Holy Spirit
You sounded the Savior's heavenly gospel
And proclaimed it in the world with a fiery tongue.
You burned all deceit to ashes like dried grass,
And throughout the universe you preached the gospel
of the Lord Christ who is the Master of all.

As Moses of old,
You were instructed by divine ascent;
Desiring to see God spiritually
You saw His Image.
You received the Son as the Knowledge and Witness of
the Father,

[3]See Heb 1, Jn 1:17-18.

[4]See Jn 1:1-18; Phil 2:6-11; Col 1:15-20; Heb 1:1-3. The Revised Standard Version of the Bible translates the nouns in the third verse as verbs. It should read: "He is the Radiance of the Glory of God, the Very Stamp [or Exact Image] of His Person" (Heb 1:3).

[5]See Jn 1:1, 20:18; Phil 2:6; Heb 1:8. This is developed theologically and stated formally in the Nicene Creed.

For They are known as one Being,
The Unity honorably exalted by all:
One Kingdom, Power, Glory, and Worship.

O new wonder,
Greater than all ancient wonders,
For who has ever known a mother without a husband
To have brought forth a Child
And carried in her arms the One who holds all creation?
This Child is God's good will!
Having carried Him in your arms as an infant,
   O Pure One,
And having boldness as a mother before Him,
Intercede before Him always for those who honor you,
That our souls may receive mercy and be saved![6]

[6]Vespers of the feast of the apostle Philip.

3

The Prelude of God's Good Will

During the first days of the Christmas fast the Church celebrates the feast of the entrance of the child Mary into the Jerusalem temple. Called in the Church The Entrance of the Most Holy Theotokos into the Temple, this festival, which is not among the biblically recorded events, is one of the twelve major feasts of the Orthodox Church year.[1] Its purpose is not so much to commemorate an historical happening as to celebrate a dogmatic mystery of the Christian faith, namely, that every human being is made to be a living temple of God.

The festal event is that the three-year-old Mary, in fulfillment of a promise made at her conception by her parents, Joachim and Anna, is offered by them to God in the temple at Jerusalem. The young child is hymned with lines taken from Psalm 45, mystically interpreted as prophetic of her vocation to be the mother of the Messiah.

Hear, O daughter, consider, and incline your ear;
forget your people and your father's house;
and the king will desire your beauty.
Since he is your lord, bow to him;
the people of Tyre will sue your favor with gifts,
the richest of the people with all kinds of wealth.

[1]The feast is celebrated on November 21, with an octave, i.e. an eight day celebration. The word Theotokos means literally "the one who gives birth to God." It is a title for Mary which was confirmed by the Third Ecumenical Council in Ephesus in 433 and was repeated by later councils. It affirms the Orthodox dogma that the One born of Mary as a man is the same One who is born of the Father in a divine manner before all ages: the Son of God and the Son of Mary, one and the same Son. See below, pp. 122-127.

The princess is decked in her chamber with gold-woven
    robes;
in many-colored robes she is led to the king,
with her virgin companions, her escort, in her train.
With joy and gladness they are led along
as they enter the palace of the king.
Instead of your fathers shall be your sons;
you will make them princes in all the earth.
I will cause your name to be celebrated in all generations;
therefore the peoples will praise you for ever and ever.
                                                (Ps 45:10-17)

The spiritual story tells how, coming into the temple, the child Mary is led into the Holy of Holies by the priest Zachariah, the father of John the Baptist, there to be nourished by angels in preparation for her virginal conception of the Son of God. In entering the Holy Place she brings to an end the "shadow" of the earthly, physical temple of God in order to commence the "reality" of the human, spiritual temple of His dwelling, which she herself is, and which, through her, all human beings become in Christ and the Holy Spirit in the Church.

Today, let us the faithful dance for joy,
Singing to the Lord with psalms and hymns,
Venerating His consecrated tabernacle,
The living Ark which contains the Word which cannot
    be contained.
For she, a young child, in the flesh
Is offered in wondrous fashion to the Lord,
And Zacharias the priest receives her with rejoicing
As the dwelling place of God.

Today the living temple of the holy glory of Christ our
    God,
She who alone among women is blessed and pure,
Is offered in the temple of the Law,
That she may make her dwelling in the Holy Place.
Joachim and Anna rejoice with her is spirit

And choirs of virgins sing to the Lord,
Chanting psalms and honoring His mother.

Led by the Holy Spirit,
The holy and immaculate maiden is taken to dwell in
    the holy temple.
She who is in truth the most holy temple of our holy God
Is nourished by the angels.
He has sanctified all things by her entry
And has made godlike the fallen nature of mortal man.

Today let us, the assembly of the faithful, triumph in spirit
And praise with reverence the child of God, the Virgin
    and Theotokos,
As she is offered in the temple of the Lord,
She who was forechosen from all generations
To be the dwelling place of Christ,
The Master and God of all.
O virgins bearing lamps, go before her,
Honoring the majestic advance of the ever Virgin.
O mothers, set aside every sorrow to follow them in
    gladness,
Singing the praises of her who became the Mother of God
And mediator of joy for the world.
Let us all cry to her joyfully with the angels:
"Rejoice, O Full of Grace who ever intercedes for our
    souls![2]

The feast of the entrance of the Theotokos into the temple
is called in the main hymn of the feast "the prelude of the
good will of God" announced by the angels to the world at
the birth of Christ. It is the first celebration of the salvation
which comes to the world in Jesus, of which Mary herself is
the first and foremost recipient.

Today is the prelude of the good will of God,
Of the preaching of the salvation of mankind.
The Virgin appears in the temple of God,

[2]Vespers of the feast.

In anticipation proclaiming Christ to all.
Let us rejoice and sing to her:
Rejoice, O Fulfillment of the Creator's dispensation.[3]

The most pure Temple of the Savior;
The precious Chamber and Virgin;
The sacred Treasure of the glory of God,
Is presented today to the house of the Lord.
She brings with her the grace of the Spirit,
Which the angels of God do praise.
Truly this woman is the Abode of Heaven![4]

[3]Troparion of the feast. The word "dispensation," in Greek *oikonomia,* means literally the "household plan" of God for the salvation of the world.
[4]Kontakion of the feast.

4

Temples of the Living God

In the Orthodox Church the Virgin Mary is the image of those who are being saved. If Jesus Christ is the Savior, Mary is, par excellence, the image of the *saved*. She is, in every aspect of her life, as Father Alexander Schmemann so often said, not the great *exception,* but rather the great *example.* From her conception to her dormition, that is, her true and real death, she shows how all people must be when they are sanctified by the Holy Spirit as servants of God and imitators of Christ.[1]

In the festival of the entrance of Mary into the temple we have seen how Christ's mother is continuously hymed as the "living temple of the holy glory of Christ our God." She is praised as the "living ark which contained the Word which cannot be contained." She is glorified as "the temple that is to hold God," consecrated by the Spirit to be the "dwelling place of the Almighty." She enters the Holy of Holies to become herself the "animated Holy of Holies," the one in whom Christ is formed, thereby making her, and everyone who is one with her in faith, the "abode of heaven."

O Most-holy One, honored far above the heavens,
You are both temple and palace,

[1]According to Orthodox dogmatic theology, Mary's conception by Joachim and Anna is exactly like our own. There is no need for a special intervention of God to remove the "stain" (*macula* in Latin) of original sin since no "stain" is transmitted in the act of conception. Hence the Orthodox do not have a doctrine or feast of the "immaculate conception." See below, pp. 41-44. Also, Mary's dormition or "falling asleep" is seen to be a real death, yet one that is fulfilled in her immediate resurrection and glorification, since in her the fulness of Christ's victory over death is fulfilled and celebrated.

You are dedicated in the temple of God
To be prepared as the divine dwelling place of His coming.

Let us praise the glorious entrance of the Theotokos
   in songs,
For today she is prophetically offered in the temple as
   a precious gift,
Being herself the temple of God.[2]

We are all made to be living temples of God. We are all created to be dwelling places of His glory. We are all fashioned in His image and likeness to be abodes of His presence. The first Christian martyr, the protodeacon Stephen whose memory is celebrated on the third day of Christmas, was killed for proclaiming this marvel when he bore witness that "the Most High does not dwell in houses made with hands." For this, like Jesus Himself, he was accused of planning the destruction of the earthly temple at Jerusalem (Acts 7:48; 6:14).[3] The apostle Paul proclaims this same doctrine clearly and without equivocation when he writes to the Corinthians and to us that "we are God's fellow workers; you are God's field, God's building" (1 Cor 3:9).

Do you not know that you are God's temple and that God's Spirit dwells in you? If any one destroys God's temple, God will destroy Him. For God's temple is holy, and that temple you are. (1 Cor 3:16-17)

This same teaching is found in the apostle's letter to the Ephesians as the confirmation of the words of Jesus recorded in St John's gospel, that "if a man loves Me, he will keep My word, and My Father will love him, and We will come to him and make Our home with him" (Jn 14:23).

. . . for through Him [Christ] we both [Jews and Gentile] have access in one Spirit to the Father. So then you are no longer strangers and sojourners, but you

---

[2]Matins of the feast.
[3]See Jn 2:19-21; Mt 26:61, 27:40. Also see below, pp. 131-135.

are fellow citizens with the saints and members of the household of God, built upon the foundation of the apostles and prophets, Christ Jesus Himself being the cornerstone, in whom the whole structure is joined together and grows into a holy temple in the Lord; in whom you also are built into it for a dwelling place of God in the Spirit. (Eph 2:18-22)[4]

Jesus Christ, the Son, Word, and Image of God, is physically and spiritually formed in the body of Mary so that He might be formed in us as well (see Gal 4:19). This is the meaning of Christmas, which is the meaning of life itself: Christ in us and we in Christ, God with us and we with God. The Spirit in our hearts so that the Spirit can flow out from us, sanctifying the world around us. This is not mere symbolism, the high-blown language of the liturgy and the scriptures. This is serious business. It is a matter of life and death. For we are either the living vessels of God—"earthen vessels" to be sure, to show, as the apostle again affirms, that "the transcendent power belongs to God and not to us" (2 Cor 4:7)—or we are, to use the apostle's language once more, "vessels of wrath" to be destroyed in our wickedness by God's righteous glory (Rom 9:22).

As we go the way of the Winter Pascha the choice placed before us is clear. We can follow the "narrow way" that leads to life, or we can go on the "broad way" that leads to destruction (Mt 7:13-14). We can, like Mary, cleave to the Lord and become His dwelling place in the Spirit. Or we can through immorality and sin choose the death of the nothingness which we are unless the Lord Himself lives within us. "But he who is united to the Lord becomes one spirit with Him" (1 Cor 6:17).

Let the heavens above greatly rejoice
And let the clouds pour down gladness today
At the mighty acts of our God, exceedingly marvelous.
For behold, the "Gate facing the East" is born

[4]See also 1 Pet 2:4-5.

According to the promise from a fruitless and barren
    womb,
And is dedicated to God as His dwelling,
Led this day into the temple as an offering most pure.
Let David greatly rejoice, striking his harp:
"Virgins," he said, "shall be led with the queen"
Into the tabernacle of God, His place of propitiation,
There to be raised to become the dwelling place of Him
    who was begotten of the Father without change
    before all ages for the salvation of the world.[5]

[5]Vespers of the feast. The title "Gate facing the East" is ascribed by the liturgy to Mary because the Glory of the Lord entered through this gate of the Jerusalem temple, which then was forever sealed so that no mere mortal could pass there, thus symbolizing the unique birth of the Son of God from His ever-virgin mother. See Ezek 43:1-5, 44:1-4.

5

Christ Is Born, Glorify Him!

The feast of the entrance of Mary into the temple marks the first specific liturgical announcement of the birth of Christ. On this festival, for the first time in the season, the canon of the Nativity of Christ is sung at the festal vigil.[1]

Christ is born; glorify Him!
Christ comes from heaven; go to meet Him!
Christ is on earth; be exalted!
Sing to the Lord, all the earth!
And praise Him in gladness, O people,
For He has been glorified!

To the Son, begotten of the Father before all ages,
And incarnate of the Virgin without seed in these latter
    days—
To Christ our God let us cry out:
You have raised up our horn.
Holy are You, O Lord!

Stem and flower of the root of Jesse,
You have blossomed from the Virgin, O Christ.
From the mountain overshadowed by the forest You
    have come,
Made flesh from her who knew no man.
O God not formed from matter—
Glory to Your power, O Lord!

[1]The Christmas canon is sung at the vigil of the feast of the Entrance of the Theotokos as the second canon of matins. It is customary to sing it at each major vigil after this feast until Christmas itself.

I behold a strange, most glorious mystery!
Heaven—the cave!
The cherubic throne—the Virgin!
The manager—the place where Christ lay,
The uncontainable God whom we magnify in song.[2]

The Christmas canon, nine odes following the biblical canticles of Moses, Hannah, Habbakuk, Isaiah, Jonah, the three young men in the Babylonian furnace, and the magnificat of the Virgin herself, was inspired by a famous homily for the festival of Christ's birth given in the fourth century by Saint Gregory Nazianzen who is called in Orthodox tradition the Theologian. The friend of Saint Basil the Great and defender of the divinity of the Son and Word of God, and therefore of the dogma of the Most Holy Trinity, Gregory is praised not only as a great theologian and mystical poet, but as a great preacher of the Christian life. These are passages from the sermon which has been incorporated into the liturgical songs of the Church in her celebration of the Winter Pascha:

Christ is born, glorify Him. Christ from heaven, go to meet Him. Christ on earth, be lifted up. Sing to the Lord, all the earth. And that I may join the two in one word: Let the heavens rejoice, and let the earth be glad, because of Him who is of heaven and is now on earth. Christ in the flesh, rejoice with trembling and with joy; with trembling because of your sins, and with joy because of your hope. Christ of a virgin. Live as virgins, you mothers, that you may be mothers of Christ. Who does not worship Him who is from the beginning? Who does not glorify Him who is also the End?

Again the darkness is past. Again Light is made. . . . The people that sat in darkness, let them see the Great Light of full knowledge. Old things have passed away. Behold, all things are becoming new. The letter

---

[2]Matins of the feast of the Entrance and of the Nativity.

gives way, and the Spirit come to the fore. The shadows
flee away, for the Truth has come upon them. Mel-
chisedec is now fulfilled. He that was without a mother
(being begotten from the Father before the ages) now
becomes without a father (being born of the Virgin).
The laws of nature are upset. The world above must
be filled. Christ commands it. Let us not set ourselves
against Him.

Clap your hands together, all people. For unto us
a Son is born, unto us a Child is given, and the government shall be upon His shoulders. . . . Let John the
Baptist cry aloud: Prepare ye the way of the Lord!
And I too will cry aloud about the power of this Day.
He who is without flesh has become incarnate. The Son
of God becomes the Son of man. Jesus Christ: the same
yesterday and today and forever! Let the children of
Israel who seek signs be scandalized. Let the Greeks
who seek wisdom speak of folly.[3] Let all the heretics
talk till their tongues ache. They shall believe when
they see Him ascending up into the heavens. And if
not then, when they see Him coming out of the heavens
to sit in judgment.

But this is not for now. For the present let us speak
of the festival which is called both the Nativity and
the Theophany. For it is called both, two titles belong
to the same thing. For God was manifested to man by
birth. On the one hand He is *Being*, eternally Being
of the Eternal Being [God from God], above every
cause and word; for the Word of God is before every
word. And on the other hand for our sake He is also
Becoming, so that He who gives us our being might
also give us our well-being; or rather that He might
restore us by His incarnation when we have by our
wickedness fallen from well-being. The name Theophany is given to the feast in reference to the Manifestation [for in Greek *theophany* means "manifestation
of God"]; and that of Nativity is in respect to His
Birth.

[3]See 1 Cor 1:22-23.

This then is our present festival. It is this that we
are celebrating today: the Coming of God to man,
that we might go forth, or rather (for this is the more
proper expression), that we might go back to God—
that putting off the old man we might put on the
New; and that as we have died in Adam so we might
live in Christ, being born with Christ and crucified
with Him and buried with Him and rising with
Him. . . .

Therefore, let us keep the feast, not after the
manner of a pagan festival, but in a godly way. Not
after the way of this world, but in the fashion of the
world which is above. Not as something our own, but
as that which belongs to Him who is ours, or rather,
as our Master's. Not as of weakness, but as of healing.
Not as of creation, but of re-creation.

And how shall this be? Let us not decorate our
porches, nor arrange dances, nor adorn the streets. Let
us not feast with the eyes, nor enchant the ears with
music, nor enervate the nostrils with perfume, nor
prostitute the taste, nor indulge the touch. These are
the ways that lead to evil and are the entrances of sin.
. . . Let us leave all these things to the pagans . . . But
let us who are worshippers of the Word of God, if
we must in some way have luxury, let us seek it in
God's Word and in the law and the scriptural stories,
especially those which tell us of the present festival
so that our pleasure may be like unto Him who has
called us together today.

. . . for He who gives riches becomes poor, for
He assumes the povery of my flesh that I may assume
the riches of His divinity. He that is full empties Himself, for He empties Himself of His glory for a short
while that I may have a share in His fullness. What
are the riches of His goodness! What is this mystery
that is around me! I had a share in the Image but I
did not keep it. He now partakes of my flesh that He
might both save the image and make the flesh immortal. He communicates a Second Communion [in

the incarnation] far more marvelous than the First
[in creation]. For in creation He gave us a share of
His own good nature. And now in the Nativity He
takes on Himself our own sinful one. The Nativity is
a more Godlike action. It is superior in the eyes of all
people of understanding.[4]

[4]Gregory Nazianzen, Oration 38, *On the Theophany or Nativity of Christ.*

6

The Feast of Saint Andrew

While the canon of the feast of the Nativity begins to be sung on the festival of the entrance of the Virgin Mary into the temple, the first prefeast hymns of Christmas are sung on the feast of "the all-praised and first-called apostle Andrew."[1]

In the gospel according to Saint John, Philip calls his friend Nathanael to "come and see" Jesus, but it is Jesus Himself who invites Andrew to "come and see" where He dwells and to spend the day with Him, together with another disciple of John the Baptist, who is probably the evangelist himself.

> . . . John [the Baptist] was standing with two of his disciples; and he looked at Jesus as He walked, and said, "Behold, the Lamb of God!" The two disciples heard him say this, and they followed Jesus. Jesus turned, and saw them following, and said to them, "What do you seek?" And they said to Him, "Rabbi" (which means Teacher), "where are you staying?" He said to them, "Come and see." They came and saw

[1]Feast of Saint Andrew, November 30. In Orthodox practice major feasts are announced by "prefeast" verses and hymns sung at services that come before the great feast. Generally speaking, nothing in Orthodox liturgical celebration comes unprepared and unannounced. And it is never the case that the faithful "pretend" that they do not know what will happen. For example, on Holy Friday it is clearly proclaimed in the worship of the crucified Lord that He will rise from the dead. The Cross is contemplated and the dead Christ is adored in the light of the resurrection. The liturgy of the Church is never a "historical representation." It is rather the mystical experience of each act of sacred history in the light of the whole, including the glorification of Christ and the outpouring of the Holy Spirit.

where He was staying; and they stayed with Him that
day, for it was about the tenth hour. One of the two
who heard John speak, and followed Him, was Andrew, Simon Peter's brother. He first found his brother
Simon, and said to him, "We have found the Messiah"
(which means Christ). (Jn 1:35-41).

Come and see! This is the abiding invitation of the Church
in her liturgical services. Come with faith and you will be
numbered with those to whom "it has been given to know
the secrets of the kingdom of heaven" (Mt 13:11). You will
be found with those to whom insight has been granted into
"the mystery of Christ" which is "the mystery hidden for
ages in God who created all things" which is now made
manifest "through the Church" even to the angels (Eph 3:4,
9-10).[2]

Come and see! You will witness the mystery of Christ's
birth from the Virgin, His manifestation at the Jordan in His
baptism by John, His victory over the devil in the desert, His
proclamation of good news to the poor, His announcement
of liberty to the oppressed, His declaration of the acceptable
year of the Lord's grace. You will witness His accomplishment of the signs of His messiahship: the blind see, the lame
walk, the deaf hear, the dumb talk. You will see the winds
cease and the seas calmed. You will behold the table spread
"in the wilderness" in the feeding of the multitudes (Ps
78:19). You will witness the casting out of demons. And,
most glorious of all, you will see the dead being raised by
the word of His power. You will know indeed that "the
kingdom of God has come upon you" (Mt 12:28), and you
will testify truly that "something greater than Jonah" and
"something greater than Solomon is here" (Mt 12:41-42).
You will see what "many prophets and righteous men longed
to see . . . and did not see it, and to hear . . . and did not
hear it" (Mt 13:17). And ultimately you will see the Son
of God Himself being lifted upon the Cross in order to
give His broken body as food for His people, and His shed
blood as their drink, that their hunger and thirst for peace

[2]See also Rom 16:25; 1 Cor 2:7; Col 1:26.

and joy and righteousness, and indeed for life itself, might be forever satisfied. You will "sit at table with Abraham, Isaac, and Jacob in the kingdom of heaven" which is brought to the world by the glorified Messiah (Mt 8:11).

To go the way of the Winter Pascha is, according to Saint Gregory the Theologian, to "travel without fault through every stage and faculty of the life of Christ." It is to enter into the mysteries of the Messiah, "all of which have but one completion: my perfection and return to the first condition of Adam." It is to "see and be seen by the great God who in Trinity is worshipped and glorified, and whom we now set forth before you as clearly as the bonds of flesh permit, in Jesus Christ our Lord."[3]

The feast of Saint Andrew, with the chanting of the first of the prefeast hymns of the Nativity, marks the beginning of this paschal journey in a special way.

> When He who was proclaimed by the voice of John
>   the Forerunner,
> "The Lamb of God who takes away the sins of
>   the world,"
> Came bringing life and salvation to all the earth
> You, O holy Andrew, were the first to follow Him.
> You were offered as the first-fruits of the human race.
> You proclaimed to Peter your brother,
> "We have found the Messiah!"
> Pray that He may enlighten and save our souls.

> Rejoice, O Isaiah, and receive the Word of God.
> Prophesy to Mary the Maiden.
> She is the Burning Bush unconsumed by the fire
>   of divinity.
> Adorn yourself, O Bethlehem.
> Open your gates, O Eden.
> Enter, O Magi, and see salvation swaddled in a crib.
> Behold the star shining above the cave;

[3]Gregory Nazianzen, Oration 38, *On the Theophany or Nativity of Christ,* 16.

It announces the life-giving Lord who saves the
    human race.

Tell us, O Joseph, how you led the Virgin
Into the Bethlehem cave.
"After searching the scriptures and hearing the angel,"
    he says,
"I am certain that Mary will wondrously give birth
    to God
Whom the wise men from the East will worship,
Offering to Him their precious gifts."
O Lord, incarnate for our sake, glory to You![4]

---

[4]Vespers of the feast of Saint Andrew. In Orthodox liturgical hymns the Virgin Mary is often called the "Burning Bush." For as the bush which Moses saw was burning, but was not consumed, so Mary held in her womb the Son and Word of God, but was not destroyed by the fire of His divinity. See Exodus 3.

7

Seeing They Do Not See

If we do not come, we will never see. But it is not enough to come. We also must see.

There were many on the earth when Jesus came, but they did not see Him as the Son of God and Savior of the world. And there are many who come to the Church and still do not see. The words apply to them as to those about whom Jesus spoke when He taught them in parables: "because seeing they do not see, and hearing they do not hear, nor do they understand" (Mt 13:13).

If we ask the question, "Why is it that some can come and still not see?" the answer is given by Jesus Himself, quoting His prophet Isaiah. He says quite simply that it is a matter of *will*. Those who do not see remain blind because they *will* not see.

With them indeed is fulfilled the prophecy of Isaiah which says: "You shall indeed hear but never understand, and you shall indeed see but never perceive. For this people's heart has grown dull, and their ears are heavy of hearing, and their eyes they have closed, lest they should perceive with their eyes, and hear with their ears, and understand with their heart, and turn for Me to heal them." (Mt 13:14-15; Is 6:9-10)

The apostle Paul refers to these same lines of the prophet when he reflects in his house of arrest in Rome about the failure of God's people to receive Jesus as the promised Messiah.

When they had appointed a day for him, they [the local leaders of the Jews] came to him at his lodging in great numbers. And he expounded the matter to them from morning till evening, testifying to the kingdom of God and trying to convince them about Jesus both from the law of Moses and from the prophets. And some were convinced by what he said, while others disbelieved. So, as they disagreed among themselves, they departed, after Paul had made one statement: "The Holy Spirit was right in saying to your fathers through Isaiah the prophet: 'Go to this people, and say, You shall indeed hear but never perceive.' " (Act 28:23-26)

Jesus also teaches why people generally do not wish to see. The reason, He says, is that they love darkness rather than light because their actions are wicked (see Jn 3:19). The light exposes the truth. It allows the reality of things to be seen. The wicked flee reality. They despise the light. They prefer their own blindness, and the delusions that they themselves create. They want to make up their own version of things. They want, most specifically, to fashion their own images of themselves. They want to see themselves not as they really are, but as they wish themselves to be. And, together with this, they want a version of others which confirms their own opinions of themselves. And, most especially, they want an image of God that they can handle and manipulate to serve their deluded and illusory purposes for their own profit and pleasure. The lovers of darkness, therefore, are fundamentally liars and idolaters. They are liars about themselves and about God. They make their own gods, and then fashion themselves in the images and likenesses of the gods they have made.

The question addressed to all of us as we make our way through the Winter Pascha is the one which Jesus put to the two blind men who called out to Him for mercy. "What do you want Me to do for you?" He asks. And they respond: "Lord, let our eyes be opened." And according to the gospels, "Jesus in pity touched their eyes, and immediately they received their sight and followed Him" (Mt 20:29-34).

We too must say: Lord, let the eyes of our minds and hearts be opened. Lord, let us see. For You Yourself have said that God Your Father has sent You into the world to make this judgment, namely "that those who do not see may see, and that those who see may become blind" (Jn 9:39).

"For God so loved the world that He gave His only Son, that whoever believes in Him should not perish but have eternal life. For God sent the Son into the world, not to condemn the world, but that the world might be saved through Him. He who believes in Him is not condemned; he who does not believe is condemned already, because he has not believed in the name of the only Son of God. And this is the judgment, that the light has come into the world, and men loved darkness rather than light, because their deeds were evil. For every one who does evil hates the light, and does not come to the light, lest his deeds should be exposed. But he who does what is true comes to the light, that it may be clearly seen that his deeds have been wrought in God" (Jn 3:16-21). These are the words of Jesus.

Rejoice, O heavens!
Proclaim everywhere the glory of God!
Today the first-called apostle Andrew stands in our midst.
He was the first to obey the Lord with fervor.
United to Him, he was enkindled by His love.
He is the reflection of the Savior's love for man,
For the rays of His light enlighten those who sat in
    darkness and in the shadow of death.
We rejoice in his holy memory
For through his prayers we receive healing and
    blessings from God.

When He who is called the Morning Star,
The Radiance of the eternal Father's glory,
In His great mercy took up His abode on earth,
You, O glorious Andrew, were the first to meet Him.
For your heart was enlightened with the perfect
    splendor of His divinity.

We bless you as the herald of the apostles of Christ
    our God.
Pray that He may enlightend and save our souls.[1]

---

[1]Vespers of Saint Andrew. See Mt 4:12-16; Is 9:1-2; Heb 1:3; Rev 2:28, 22:16.

8

The Feast of Saint Nicholas

Following the feast of Saint Andrew, prefeast hymns of the Nativity are heard once again on the feast of Saint Nicholas, the fourth-century bishop of Myra in Lycia who through the ages has come to be especially connected with the festival of Christ's birth.

O you who love the festivals,
Come gather and sing the praises of the fair beauty
    of bishops,
The glory of the fathers,
The fountain of wonders and great protector of
    the faithful.
Let us all say: Rejoice, O guardian of the people of Myra,
Their head and honored counsellor,
The pillar of the Church which cannot be shaken.
Rejoice, O light full of brightness
That makes the ends of the world shine with wonders.
Rejoice, O divine delight of the afflicted,
The fervent advocate of those who suffer from injustice.
And now, O all-blessed Nicholas,
Never cease praying to Christ our God
For those who honor the festival of your memory
With faith and with love.

Make ready, O cave, for the Mother-Lamb comes
Bearing Christ in her womb.
Receive Him, O manager, who by a word released the
    dwellers on earth from all lawlessness.
You shepherds abiding in the fields,
Bear witness to the awesome wonder.

You wise men from Persia,
Offer the king your gold, frankincense, and myrrh.
For the Lord has appeared from the Virgin Mother,
And she, bending over Him as His handmaiden,
Worshipped Him as He lay in her arms, saying:
"How were You sown in me as a seed?
How have You grown in me?
My Redeemer and my God!"

O unwedded Virgin, from where have you come?
Who has given you birth?
Who is your mother?
How can you carry your Creator in your arms?
How is your womb free from corruption?
O Most Holy One,
We see great and awesome mysteries upon earth fulfilled
    in you.
We adorn the cave as a house worthy of you.
We ask the heavens to send us a star.
For behold, the wise men proceed from East to West,
Desiring to see the salvation of mortal men
Shining in your arms like a pillar of fire.[1]

Sad as it is to see Saint Nicholas transformed into the
red-suited Santa Claus of the secular winter "holidays," it
is easy to understand why the holy bishop has become so
closely connected with the festival of Christ's birth. The
stories about the saint, fabricated and embroidered in Christian
imagination over the ages, in various times and places, all
tell of the simple faith and love of the man known only for
his goodness and love.

The extraordinary thing about the image of Saint Nicholas
in the Church is that he is not known for anything extraordinary. He was not a theologian and never wrote a word,
yet he is famous in the memory of believers as a zealot for
orthodoxy, allegedly accosting the heretic Arius at the first
ecumenical council in Nicaea for denying the divinity of
God's Son. He was not an ascetic and did no outstanding feats

[1]Vespers of the feast of Saint Nicholas

of fasting and vigils, yet he is praised for his possession of the "fruit of the Holy Spirit . . . love, joy, peace, patience, kindness, goodness, faithfulness, gentleness, self-control" (Gal 5:22-23). He was not a mystic in our present meaning of the term but he lived daily with the Lord and was godly in all of his words and deeds. He was not a prophet in the technical sense, yet he proclaimed the Word of God, exposed the sins of the wicked, defended the rights of the oppressed and afflicted, and battled against every form of injustice with supernatural compassion and mercy. In a word, he was a good pastor, father, and bishop to his flock, known especially for his love and care for the poor. Most simply put, he was a divinely good person.

We use that term "goodness" so lightly in our time. How easily we say of someone, "He is a *good* man" or "She is a *good* woman." How lightly we say, "They are *good* people." A teen-age girl takes an overdose of drugs, and the neighbors tell the reporters, "But she was always such a good girl, and her parents are such nice people!" A young man commits some terrible crime, and the same rhetoric flows: "But he was always such a good boy, and his family is so nice.'" A man dies on the golf course after a life distinguished by many years of profit-taking and martini-drinking, and the reaction is the same: "He was a good man, yeah, a real nice guy." What do "good" and "nice" really mean in such cases? What do they describe? What do they express?

In Saint Luke's gospel it tells us that one day a "ruler" came up to Jesus and asked, "Good Teacher, what shall I do to inherit eternal life?" And Jesus answered him, "Why do you call Me good? No one is good but God alone" (Lk 18:18; see also Mk 10:18). In Saint Matthew's version it says that Jesus answered the man by saying, "Why do you ask Me about what is good? One there is who is good" (Mt 19:17). However we choose to interpret Christ's words, at least one point is clear. Jesus reacts to the facile, perhaps even sarcastic, use of the term "good" by referring it to its proper source. There is only One who is good, and that is God Himself. If you want to speak of goodness, then you must realize what— and Whom—you are talking about!

Like God, and like Jesus, Saint Nicholas was genuinely good. Real goodness is possible. For, to quote the Lord again, "with men this is impossible, but with God all things are possible" (Mt 19:26). A human being, even a rich human being who believes in God, can be genuinely good with God's own goodness. "For truly I say to you," says the Lord, "if you have faith as a grain of mustard seed . . . nothing will be impossible to you" (Mt 17:20-21).

The Messiah has come so that human beings can live lives which are, strictly speaking, humanly impossible. He has come so that people can really be *good.* One of the greatest and most beloved examples among believers that this is true is the holy bishop of Myra about whom almost nothing else is known, or needs to be known, except that he was good. For this reason alone he remains, even in his secularized form, the very spirit of Christmas.

O holy father,
The fruit of your good deeds has enlightened and
    delighted the hearts of the faithful.
Who cannot wonder at your measureless patience
    and humility?
At your graciousness to the poor?
At your compassion for the afflicted?
O Bishop Nicholas,
You have divinely taught all things well,
And now wearing your unfading crown, you intercede
    for our souls.[2]

You appeared to your flock as a rule of faith,
An image of humility and a teacher of abstinence.
Because of your lowliness, heaven was opened to you.
Because of your poverty, riches were granted to you.
O holy Bishop Nicholas,
Pray to Christ our God to save our souls.[3]

[2]Vespers of the feast of Saint Nicholas.
[3]Troparion of the feast of Saint Nicholas, which has become in Orthodox liturgical services the "general troparion" for most canonized bishops of the Church, thus revealing the "mind of the Church" about what a Christian pastor should be.

9

The Conception of Mary

On the ninth of December the Orthodox Church celebrates the feast of the conception of the Virgin Mary by her parents Joachim and Anna.[1] On this major festival which finds its place in the Church's preparation for Christmas, the faithful rejoice in the event by which Mary is conceived in fulfillment of her parents' prayers in order to be formed in the womb, born on the earth, dedicated to the Lord, and nurtured in holiness to become by God's grace the mother of His Son the Messiah.

In addition to the songs of the services, there are icons and frescoes of the feast which the faithful venerate and kiss, depicting the holy couple in a loving embrace within their conjugal chamber.

O Adam and Eve, lay aside your sorrow,
Behold, a barren womb today wondrously bears fruit:
The Mother of our Joy!

O Father Abraham and all the patriarchs,
Rejoice greatly, seeing your seed blossom:
The Mother of our God!

Rejoice, O Anna! Joachim, rejoice!
Today in wondrous manner you bear to the world
The fruit of grace and salvation!

[1]The feast is officially called The Conception of the Theotokos. Mary's nativity is celebrated on September 8. A popular tradition among the Orthodox says that the nine-month period is purposely off by one day to illustrate the "mere humanity" of Mary, unlike the "divine humanity" of her Son, whose conception on the feast of the Annunciation is celebrated on March 25, exactly nine months before His Nativity.

O choir of prophets, rejoice exceedingly!
For behold, today Anna bears the holy fruit
You foretold to us.

Rejoice, all nations!
The barren Anna conceives the fruit of her womb;
By persevering in hope, she bears our life!

Rejoice, O ends of the earth!
Behold the barren mother conceives her
Who without human seed will bear the Creator of all!

Today a royal robe of purple and fine linen
Is woven from the loins of David.
The mystical flower of Jesse is blossoming
From which comes Christ our God, the Savior of our souls.[2]

The Orthodox Church, particularly in the present time, does not call the feast of Mary's beginning the "immaculate conception," although perhaps in ancient times this title would have been fully acceptable.[3] This is not because the Orthodox consider Mary's conception to have been somehow "maculate" or "stained" (*macula* means "stain" in Latin). It simply means that the Orthodox do not want to support the conviction that God had somehow to intervene at the moment of Mary's conception with a special action to remove the "stain" of the original sin transmitted by the act of human reproduction because, simply put, the Orthodox do not hold that such a "stain" exists.

The Orthodox Church affirms original sin. Orthodox

---

[2]Matins of the feast of the Conception of the Theotokos.

[3]Roman Catholics celebrate the feast of the Immaculate Conception of the Virgin Mary on December 8. The "immaculate conception" is an officially promulgated dogma of the Roman Church which teaches that God applied the "merits of Christ" to Mary at the very moment of her conception so that she could be freed from the "stain" of original sin and could thereby become the most pure Mother of the Savior, the incarnate Son and Word of God. Some schools of theology teach that all human beings are guilty of the original sin because they somehow pre-existed "in Adam." Some also hold that the transmission of the stain of original sin is by way of the manner of human reproduction through sexual intercourse.

theology teaches that all human beings, including the Virgin Mary who is a "mere human" like the rest of us—unlike her Son Jesus who is a "real human" but not a "mere human" because He is the incarnate Son and Word of God—are born into a fallen, death-bound, demon-riddled world whose "form is passing away" (1 Cor 7:31). We are all born mortal and tending toward sin. But we are not born guilty of any *personal* sin, certainly not one allegedly committed "in Adam." Nor are we born stained because of the manner in which we are conceived by the sexual union of our parents. If sexual union in marriage is in any sense sinful, or the cause in itself of any sinfulness or stain, even in the conditions of the "fallen world," then, as even the rigorous Saint John Chrysostom has taught, God is the sinner because He made us this way, male and female, from the very beginning.[4]

The Orthodox Church teaches that it is possible by the grace of God, with whom all things are possible, for sexual union in marriage, even in the present condition of things, to be good, holy, beautiful, loving, and pure. The proof of this is the feast of Joachim and Anna's conception of Mary (and Zacharias and Elizabeth's conception of John the Baptist), with no mention whatsoever of any "stain" having to be removed by a special action of God, certainly not one connected with the manner in which the conception occurs.[5]

Mary is conceived by her parents as we are all conceived. But in her case it is a pure act of faith and love, in obedience to God's will, as an answer to prayer. In this sense her conception is truly "immaculate." And its fruit is the woman who remains forever the most pure Virgin and Mother of God.

> Come, let us dance in the Spirit!
> Let us sing worthy praises to Christ!
> Let us celebrate the joy of Joachim and Anna,

[4]See John Chrysostom, *On Titus*, homily 2.

[5]The Orthodox Church celebrates the feast of The Conception of the Holy Prophet, Forerunner, and Baptist John on September 23. His nativity is celebrated on June 24; again the nine-month period is off by one day. (See above, note 1). A movement existed among some Roman Catholics at the beginning of this century which unsuccessfully argued that the church should teach the "immaculate conception" of Saint John.

The conception of the Mother of our God,
For she is the fruit of the grace of God.[6]

Anna besought the Lord in fervent prayer for a child.
The voice of the angel proclaimed to her:
God has granted you the desire of your prayer.
Do not weep, for you shall be a fruitful vine,
Bearing the wondrous branch of the Virgin
Who will bring forth in the flesh the blossom Christ,
Who grants great mercy to the world.

Today the great mystery of all eternity,
Whose depths angels and men cannot perceive,
Appears in the barren womb of Anna.
Mary, the Maiden of God, is prepared to be the dwelling
     place of the eternal King
Who will renew human nature.
Let us entreat her with a pure heart and say:
Intercede for us with your Son and God
That our souls may be saved.[7]

---

[6]Prefeast hymn at vespers of December 8, the prefeast of the Conception of the Theotokos.

[7]Vespers of the feast of the Conception of the Theotokos.

10

The Feast of Saint Herman

The elder Herman of Alaska, missionary monk of Spruce Island near Kodiak, died on the thirteenth of December in 1837. He is the first formally canonized saint of the Orthodox Church in America.[1] The feast day of his death now forms a central part of the liturgical celebration of the Winter Pascha for Orthodox Christians living in North America.

O joyful North Star of the Church of Christ,
Guiding all men to the heavenly kingdom.
O Teacher and Apostle of the true faith,
Intercessor and defender of the oppressed.
Adornment of the Orthodox Church in America,
Blessed Father Herman of Alaska,
Pray to our Lord Jesus Christ for the salvation of our
    souls.[2]

For those familiar with the actions of the Lord in history, who have heard of the passover of His people from Egypt, who have been struck by the Word of God from the mouth of His prophets, who have believed in the gospel of the Kingdom of His incarnate Word Jesus, the fact that the elder Herman should be the first glorified saint in His Church in America comes as no surprise whatsoever. How like the Lord it is—who has His only-begotten Son born on earth of a lowly woman in a cavern, nailed to the Cross with thieves outside the walls of the Holy City, witnessed in His resurrection by a

[1]Saint Herman was officially canonized as a saint of the Church on August 9, 1970. This day is also an annual feast of the holy father.
[2]Troparion of the feast of Saint Herman.

45

former prostitute out of whom came seven devils, and preached by the greatest apostle who had previously acted as an accomplice to the murder of the first Christian martyr—how like this Lord it is to raise up first among the holy ones of the Church in the new lands a person like Saint Herman.

The young monk Herman was a hermit in the monastery of Valaamo in Russian Finland. He was chosen to be a member of the first missionary team being sent to the Russian lands in Alaska. He was not ordained. He was not formally educated. He had no particular human skills. His only grace was that he was a holy man, a person of genuine faith and continuous prayer.

Herman came to America with the first group of missionaries. He alone survived, living for many years as a simple monk on Spruce Island. He taught the people the gospel. He attended to their spiritual and physical needs. He defended them against the cruelty of the Russian traders. He pleaded their cause before the imperial throne. He was beaten and persecuted by his own people for his condemnation of their injustices and sins. He identified wholly with the afflicted and oppressed. He died in obscurity, foretelling his glorification in future years by the Church that would emerge from his own humble efforts and those of the waves of immigrants who would inhabit the continent. And he revealed himself from heaven to those who, like him, remained faithful to God, including the great missionary bishop, the widowed priest and "apostle to America," Saint Innocent Veniaminoff.[3]

American Christianity desperately needs the witness of Saint Herman, for the American way of life is so radically opposed in so many ways to the life of this man and the Lord Jesus whom he served. Power, possessions, profits, pleasures: these are the things that Americans are known for. These are the goals that we are schooled to pursue. These are the things in which we take pride. And, sadly enough, these are also the

[3]John Veniaminoff was a married priest who went to Alaska as a missionary in 1824. After his wife's death, he was tonsured a monk with the name of Innocent and was made a bishop. He died in 1879 as the metropolitan of Moscow, the head of the Russian Orthodox Church. He was officially canonized a saint on October 6, 1977, which day remains his annual feast, together with March 31, the day of his death.

things that many of us are taught to value by our "religious leaders," both by their words and their examples. But this was is not the way of the Lord Jesus Christ. And it is not the way of His saints.

> Do not lay up for yourselves treasures on earth, where moth and rust consume and where thieves break in and steal, but lay up for yourselves treasure in heaven, where neither moth nor rust consumes and where thieves do not break in and steal. For where your treasure is, there will your heart be also. . . . No one can serve two masters; for either he will hate the one and love the other, or he will be devoted to the one and despise the other. You cannot serve God and mammon. Therefore I tell you, do not be anxious about your life, what you shall eat or what you shall drink, nor about your body, what you shall put on. Is not life more than food, and the body more than clothing? . . . Therefore do not be anxious, saying, "What shall we eat?" or "What shall we drink?" or "What shall we wear?" For the Gentiles seek all these things; and your heavenly Father knows that you need them all. But seek first His kingdom and His righteousness, and all these things shall be yours as well. (Mt 6:19-21, 24-25, 31-33)

By American standards, Saint Herman of Alaska, like the Lord Jesus Himself, was a miserable failure. He made no name for himself. He was not in the public eye. He wielded no power. He owned no property. He had few possessions, if any at all. He had no worldly prestige. He played no role in human affairs. He partook of no carnal pleasures. He made no money. He died in obscurity among outcast people. Yet today, more than a hundred years after his death, his icon is venerated in thousands of churches and his name is honored by millions of people whom he is still trying to teach to seek the kingdom of God and its righteousness which has been brought to the world by the King who was born in a cavern

and killed on a cross. The example of this man is crucial to
the celebration of Christmas—especially in America.

> The Orthodox Church in America
> Calls all to join in her praise of your wondrous work,
> O blessed Father Herman!
> You have attained rest from your holy labors in the
>   heavenly mansions.
> We are filled with wonder by your exemplary life.
> Intercede for us before Christ our God
> That He may grant peace to our souls.
> You gave your whole life to God,
> Having love for Him above all,
> Desiring only the converse of heaven,
> You did not forsake the love of your brothers, O Saint,
> Praying and singing together with them:
> O sweetest Jesus, grant Your salvation to us sinners.[4]

> O blessed Father Herman of Alaska,
> North Star of Christ's holy Church,
> The light of your holy life and great deeds
> Guides those who follow the Orthodox way.
> Together we lift high the holy Cross
> You planted firmly in America.
> Let all behold and glorify Jesus Christ,
> Singing His holy Resurrection.[5]

---

[4]Matins of the feast of Saint Herman.
[5]A second troparion of the feast of Saint Herman.

11

Father Alexander's Winter Pascha

Father Alexander Schmemann was the dean of Saint Vladimir's Seminary in Crestwood, New York, and the spiritual father, teacher, pastor, and friend of countless people not only in America but around the world. He died on December 13, 1983, the same day of the year as Saint Herman of Alaska. For those who knew him, and those who will yet come to know him, the day of Father Alexander's death will always be a precious part of the Church's celebration of the Christmas-Epiphany season.

As we have already noted, the expression "Winter Pascha" was coined by Father Alexander.[1] The Church's Typikon speaks of the celebration of the Lord's Coming in the flesh as a "splendid Pascha." It was Father Alexander who added the adjective "winter" for those of us who celebrate it in the darkness of wintertime, when the light is just starting to shine more brightly and the nights begin to shorten, heralding the victory of Light and Life in the springtime Pascha of the Lord's Death and Resurrection.

Father Alexander learned that he had cancer in the fall of 1982. He greeted the disease as the opportunity for Christian witness. As a person who spoke so much about Christ, he said, it was fitting that he be put to the test to confirm in action, by God's grace and power, all that he had proclaimed in words. The disease was God's gift to him of the possibility to practice what he himself had preached so forcefully and so enthusiastically for so long.

Father Alexander underwent his personal "Winter Pascha" in December of 1983 as he "passed over from death into

[1]See above, p. 11.

life," in what Mrs. Schmemann, in her letter to the seminary community, called, the "feast of Father's dying."

> Truly, truly I say to you, he who hears My word, and believes in Him who sent Me, has eternal life; he does not come into judgment, but has passed from death to life. (Jn 5:24)

On Thursday, December 8, Father Alexander received Holy Communion and was annointed in the sacrament of Holy Unction in his hospital bed in New York City. At the end of the service, when he kissed the Cross of Christ, and the priest and people said, "Amen!" Father Alexander pronounced loudly and clearly: "Amen! Amen! Amen!" This triple amen comes from the celebration of the holy Eucharist when, after the invocation of the Holy Spirit, the offered Gifts are changed into the Body and Blood of the Lord.

> Again we offer unto Thee this reasonable and bloodless worship, and ask Thee, and pray Thee, and supplicate Thee: Send down Thy Holy Spirit upon us and upon these Gifts here offered. . . .
> And make this Bread the precious Body of Thy Christ. Amen!
> And that which is in this Cup, the precious Blood of Thy Christ. Amen!
> Making the change by Thy Holy Spirit. Amen! Amen! Amen![2]

Father Alexander received Holy Communion for the last time on Sunday, December 11, the Sunday of the Holy Forefathers.[3] After partaking of the Holy Mysteries, now at home, Father listened to his family and friends sing the prefeast hymns of Christmas which he especially loved. When the praying and singing was over, he said simply, "Thank you."

On Monday morning, December 12, because of a mistake

---

[2]The eucharistic prayer of the liturgy of St John Chrysostom (translation of the Orthodox Church in America, 1967).

[3]See below, pp. 62-65.

in the official church calendar of the Orthodox Church in America, the liturgy for the feast of St Herman was celebrated in the seminary chapel. Later that morning Father Alexander was seated in a chair in his room and listened to the hymns and prayers of the Church's office of The Separation of Soul and Body. He was blessed once more with the consecrated Oil used for the mystery of Holy Unction, and lay again on the bed in which he was to die.

It stormed in Crestwood from Sunday to Tuesday, December 13. It was dark. The wind howled. There was thunder and lightning. The sidewalks and roads were flooded. Branches of trees were strewn all over. Father Alexander gave up his spirit to the Lord on Tuesday afternoon, surrounded by family and friends. Metropolitan Theodosius arrived minutes after Father passed on, and a memorial service was sung over his body, which was immediately prepared and vested and taken to the seminary chapel, there to begin the splendid celebration of Father Alexander's "Winter Pascha."

Thousands of people came. More than a hundred priests and bishops assisted. The seminary choir sang, with all of the faithful. Archbishop Iakovos of the Greek Orthodox Archdiocese and Metropolitan Philip of the Antiochian Orthodox Archdiocese, among others, spoke at the services. In response to Metropolitan Theodosius' sermon at the end of the divine liturgy on Friday, December 16, the entire body of the faithful proclaimed: "Amen! Amen! Amen!" *Amen* to the will of God. And *Amen* to the life and death of Father Alexander!

The day of Father's funeral was sunny and cloudless. Everyone remarked that it was like the Lord's Pascha in the spring. And everyone experienced, in hearing Father Alexander's own words which were read at the divine liturgy, what Pascha always means for those who believe.

> The purpose of Christianity is not to help people by reconciling them with death, but to reveal the Truth about life and death in order that people may be saved by this Truth. . . . If the purpose of Christianity were to take away from man the fear of death, to reconcile

him with death, there would be no need for Christianity, for other religions have done this, indeed, better than Christianity.[4]

The Church is the entrance into the risen life of Christ; it is communion in life eternal, "joy and peace in the Holy Spirit." And it is the expectation of the "day without evening" of the Kingdom; not of any "other world," but of the fulfillment of all things and all life in Christ. In Him death itself has become an act of life, for He has filled it with Himself, with His love and light. In Him "all things are yours; whether . . . the world, or life, or death, or things present, or things to come; all are yours; and ye are Christ's; and Christ is God's (1 Cor 3:21-23). And if I make this *new life* mine, mine this hunger and thirst for the Kingdom, mine this expectation of Christ, mine the certitude that Christ is Life, then my very death will be an act of communion with Life. For neither life nor death can separate us from the love of Christ. I do not know when and how the fulfillment will come. I do not know when all things will be consummated in Christ. I know nothing about the "whens" and "hows." But I know that in Christ this great Passage, the *Pascha* of the world has begun, that the light of the "world to come" comes to us in the joy and peace of the Holy Spirit, for *Christ is risen and Life reigneth.*

Finally I know that it is this faith and this certitude that fill with a joyful meaning the words of St Paul which we read each time we celebrate the "passage" of a brother, his falling asleep in Christ:

For the Lord himself will descend from heaven with a cry of command, with the archangel's call, and with the sound of the trumpet of God. And the dead in Christ will rise first;

[4]Alexander Schmemann, *For the Life of the World* (Crestwood, NY: St Vladimir's Seminary Press, 1973) p. 99.

then we who are alive, who are left, shall be
caught up together with them in the clouds to
meet the Lord in the air; and so we shall always
be with the Lord (I Thess. 4:16-17).[5]

[5]*For the Life of the World,* p. 106.

12

Daniel and the Three Young Men

During the prefeast season of Christmas the Church celebrates the memory of many of the Hebrew prophets. Especially commemorated are the prophet Daniel and his companions, Hananiah, Azariah, and Mishael, the three Hebrew youths who refused to worship the idol of King Nebuchadnezzar in Babylon and were thrown into a fiery furnace, only to find themselves singing and dancing in the flames together with a "fourth person" who is taken by the Church to be the prefiguration of Jesus Himself.[1]

> Because the king's order was strict and the furnace was very hot, the flame of the fire slew those men who took up Shadrach, Meshach, and Abednego. And these three men . . . fell bound into the burning fiery furnace. Then King Nebuchadnezzar was astonished and rose up in haste. He said to his counselors, "Did we not cast three men bound into the fire?" They answered the king, "True, O king." He answered, "But I see four men loose, walking in the midst of the fire, and they are not hurt; and the appearance of the fourth is like a son of the gods." (Dan 3:22-25)

The festival of Daniel and the three young men is essentially a festival of faith in the one true God, the Lord of

[1]The feast of Daniel and the Three Young Men is kept on December 17. The book of Daniel frequently uses the Babylonian names for the four: Daniel was called Belteshazzar; Hananiah, Shadrach; Mishael, Meshach; Azariah, Abednego. In classical iconography the "fourth person" in the furnace is depicted as Jesus bearing great wings and entitled "the great counsel of the angels" from the prophecy of Isaiah (see Dan 3 and Is 9).

Israel who saves those who believe in Him, and who at the
end of the ages will bring forth an everlasting kingdom to
which even the pagan kings will be compelled to bear witness.
Thus, at the end of his life Nebuchadnezzar himself is forced
to testify of the God of the three youths who put him to shame.

> At the end of the days I, Nebuchadnezzar, lifted my
> eyes to heaven, and my reason returned to me, and I
> blessed the Most High, and praised and honored Him
> who lives for ever; for His dominion is an everlasting
> dominion, and His kingdom endures from generation
> to generation; all the inhabitants of the earth are ac-
> counted as nothing; and He does according to His will
> in the host of heaven and among the inhabitants of
> the earth; and none can stay His hand or say to Him,
> "What doest Thou?" (Dan 4:34-35)

King Darius, too, was brought to proclaim the one true
God Most High when Daniel emerged untouched from the
lion's den in which the king had sealed him, saying, "May
your God, whom you serve continually, deliver you!" (Dan
6:16).

> Then King Darius wrote to all the peoples, nations,
> and languages that dwell in all the earth: "Peace be
> multiplied to you. I make a decree, that in all my royal
> dominion men tremble and fear before the God of
> Daniel, for He is the living God, enduring for ever;
> His kingdom shall never be destroyed, and His domin-
> ion shall be to the end. He delivers and rescues, He
> works signs and wonders in heaven and on earth, He
> who has saved Daniel from the power of the lions."
> (Dan 6:25-27)

The prophet Daniel was an apocalyptic seer whose visions
are repeated in the New Testament book of Revelation, where
the everlasting kingdom of God which he foretold is clearly
identified with the kingdom of the Messiah-Christ, who is
Jesus of Nazareth.

As I looked, thrones were placed and one that was
ancient of days took his seat; his raiment was white
as snow, and the hair of his head like pure wool; his
throne was fiery flames, its wheels were burning fire.
A stream of fire issued and came forth from before
him; a thousand thousands served him, and ten thousand times ten thousand stood before him; the court
sat in judgment, and the books were opened. . . .I saw
in the night visions, and behold, with the clouds of
heaven there came one like a son of man, and he
came to the Ancient of Days and was presented before
him. And to him was given dominion and glory and
kingdom, that all peoples, nations, and languages
should serve him; his dominion is an everlasting dominion, which shall not pass away, and his kingdom one
that shall not be destroyed. (Dan 7:9-10, 13-14)

As Christians celebrate the Winter Pascha they rejoice in
the men of faith and vision who prophesied the coming of
Christ, who Himself before Pilate prophesied that "hereafter
you will see the Son of man seated at the right hand of Power,
and coming on the clouds of heaven" (Mt 26:64). This is
Jesus the King from whom "the saints of the Most High shall
receive the kingdom, and possess the kingdom for ever, for
ever and ever" (Dan 7:18).

Today the prophet Daniel has gathered us in spirit,
    O faithful,
And bountifully sets a table of virtues
Before rich and poor, natives and strangers.
He offers a spiritual cup pouring forth a stream of
    devotion
Which rejoices the hearts of the faithful
And gives the grace of the Spirit.
For this prophet, the most radiant lamp who enlightens
    the world,
Has destroyed the Babylonian idols
And stopped the mouths of savage beasts.
Together with him we acclaim the three young men;

Not being gold by nature, they were shown as more
    proven then gold,
For the fire of the furnace did not melt them
But kept unharmed those surrounded by burning naptha,
    wood, and pitch!
May the Lord who has brought us to this season of the year
Grant that we may also reach the supreme and holy day of
    the Lord's Nativity,
For through their prayers, He grants us cleansing of sin
    and great mercy.

Come, let us faithfully celebrate in advance the birth
    of Christ.
And with our minds offer a song like the star to the
    wise men.
Let us cry out with praises together with the shepherds:
The deliverance of the people has come forth from a
    Virgin's womb,
And He calls the faithful.[2]

---

[2]Vespers of the feast of Daniel and the Three Young Men.

13

The Faith of the Three Young Men

The story of the three young men in Babylon is especially loved in Orthodox liturgy. Not only is there the celebration of these Hebrew youths together with Daniel eight days before the feast of the Nativity, but their story is remembered and hymned on the two Sundays before Christmas which are dedicated to the memory of all the righteous of the Old Covenant who prepared the coming of Christ.[1] In addition, the story of the three young men is read in its entirety, together with the recitation of their prayer before entering the flames and the chanting of their canticle from the depth of the furnace, at the vigil of the Lord's Pascha of the Cross and Resurrection in the spring. And at every Lord's Day vigil throughout the entire church year, the young men are hymned in the seventh and eighth odes of the resurrectional canons at matins and their canticle is prescribed to be sung.

The story of the three young men is critically important for many reasons, chief of which is their uncompromising faith in the one true God, the Lord of Israel, and their testimony to what genuine faith in God must be. How different was their expression of faith compared to what many people today think faith ought to be!

Nowadays there are many, even among Christians, who say that to have genuine faith in God is to make claims on the Lord, to be assured of His actions on behalf of the earthly well-being of His people and to count on His deliverance in very human ways. They say that those who do not express their faith in this way are actually weak in faith, doubting the

[1]See below, p. 62-70.

58

divine promises of the Lord. But such an attitude, sometimes referred to as the "name it and claim it' approach to faith in God, has nothing in common with the faith of the three holy children.

The three young men who were confronted by the wicked king of Babylon did not claim that the true God would save them from death in the flames. They surely believed that He could, but they did not insist that He would! Just the contrary. They bore witness to the fact that their God does whatever He wants. It was none of their business what He would or would not do, and it was certainly not the business of the king. They trusted their God in everything. If it was His will to deliver them, they were ready for that. But if it was His will that they should perish in the flames, they were ready for that as well! For they believed that whatever God did, He was still the God in whom they could trust for their ultimate victory. And no matter what God did, they still, under whatever circumstances, would not worship the idol that Nebuchadnezzar had set up. In a word, according to the witness of the three young men, real faith and genuine trust in God makes no deals and no claims. It is completely and totally ready, as was shown supremely in Jesus, to accept whatever the Father wills and provides, knowing that His faithful ones will never be put to shame. Only such faith can change fire into dew and deliver from death.

> Then Nebuchadnezzar in furious rage commanded that Shadrach, Meshach, and Abednego be brought. Then they brought these men before the king. Nebuchadnezzar said to them, "Is it true, O Shadrach, Meshach, and Abednego, that you do not serve my gods or worship the golden image which I have set up? Now if you are ready when you hear the sound of the horn, pipe, lyre, trigon, harp, bagpipe, and every kind of music, to fall down and worship the image which I have made, well and good; but if you do not worship, you shall immediately be cast into a burning fiery furnace; and who is the god that will deliver you out of my hands?"

Shadrach, Meshach, and Abednego answered the king, "O Nebuchadnezzar, we have no need to answer you in this matter. If it be so, our God whom we serve is able to deliver us from the burning fiery furnace; and He will deliver us out of your hand, O king. But if not, be it known to you, O king, that we will not serve your gods or worship the golden image which you have set up." (Dan 3:13-18)

The three young men in the Babylonian furnace remain forever the witnesses of true faith in the true God. They prefigure, in their total obedience, the trust of Him who "in the days of His flesh . . . offered up prayers and supplications, with loud cries and tears, to Him who was able to save Him from death, and He was heard for His godly fear." This is Jesus, who "although He was a Son, . . . learned obedience through what He suffered; and being made perfect . . . became the source of eternal salvation to all who obey Him . . ." (Heb 5:7-9). This is the only faith worthy of those who serve the living God who saves the world through the shameful death of His royal Son.

> Enkindled by the divine flame,
> The youths despised the fire,
> And in it the holy ones were bedewed
> As they formed a choir shining most brightly,
> Singing the song of many praises.
> For the all-wise and glorious ones
> Longed for the truly everlasting and indestructible
>   kingdom.[2]

> O thrice-blessed ones,
> You did not worship the image made by man,
> But armed with the invisible power of God
> You were glorified by a trial of fire.
> From the midst of the unbearable flames you called
>   upon God:

[2]Vespers of the feast of Daniel and the three young men.

"Hasten, O Compassionate One!
Come speedily to our defense
For You are merciful, and are able to accomplish
   all that You will.[3]

---

[3]Kontakion of the feast of Daniel and the three young men.

14

The Sunday of the Holy Forefathers

Two Sundays before the celebration of Christmas, the Orthodox Church rejoices in the festival of the holy forefathers of the Old Covenant, including those who came before the giving of the Law. They foretold the coming of the Messiah and are redeemed by His saving Pascha. Together with the canon of the Nativity of Christ, the following hymns are sung at the services of the day.

Let us offer praise to the fathers
Who shone forth before and during the Law;
With righteous minds they served the Lord and Master
Who shone forth from the Virgin,
And now they delight in the unending Light.

Let us honor Adam, the first-formed man and forefather
    of all,
Who was honored by the hands of the Creator.
He rests in the heavenly mansions with all the elect.

You accepted Abel as he brought forward a gift
With a most noble soul, O God and Lord of all,
And when in days of old he was murdered by a
    bloodguilty hand,
As a divine martyr You brought him before the Light.

Seth's favor with the Creator is sung throughout the world,
For with a blameless life and disposition of soul
He served Him truly.

Now in the Land of the Living he cries aloud:
"Holy are You, O Lord!"

With his whole mouth, tongue, and heart,
The wondrous Enoch hoped that in the Spirit
He might call with godly mind upon God, the
    Master of all.
Having lived on earth in a well-pleasing manner,
He has been taken up in glory.

Let us hear the divine words of those who cry aloud,
Telling of the coming of the Christ.
For behold, He is born in a cave of an unwedded Maiden,
And His awesome birth is foretold to the Wise Men
By the suddenly appearing star.[1]

The songs of the liturgical services of the day sing of
Noah, Samson, Barak, Jepthah, Nathan, Eleazar, Josiah, Job,
Samuel, David, and his son Solomon, Elijah and all the
prophets, including once again Daniel and the three holy
children. It sings also of the holy women made "strong in
the days of old by the might of Your strength, O Lord:
Hannah, Judith and Deborah; Hulda, Jael, Esther and Sarah;
Miriam the sister of Moses; Rachel, Rebecca and Ruth, the
noble-minded ones."[2] It sings, in a word, of all of the righteous of the Old Covenant times, men and women, Hebrews
and non-Hebrews, who found life in God and so, as the epistle
reading of the day proclaims and as the Church believes, "will
appear with Him in glory" when "Christ who is our life
appears" (Col 3:4).

When Christ who is our life appears, then you also
will appear with Him in glory. Put to death therefore what is earthly in you: fornication, impurity,
passion, evil desire, and covetousness, which is idolatry.

---

[1]Matins of the Sunday of the Holy Forefathers. It is interesting to note
that in a church outside Constantinople there is a huge mosaic of Christ in
glory bearing the inscription: The Land of the Living.
[2]Matins of the Sunday of the Holy Forefathers.

On account of these the wrath of God is coming. In these you once walked, when you lived in them. But now put them all away: anger, wrath, malice, slander, and foul talk from your mouth. Do not lie to one another, seeing that you have put off the old nature with its practices and have put on the new nature, which is being renewed in knowledge after the image of its creator. Here there cannot be Greek and Jew, circumcised and uncircumcised, barbarian, Scythian, slave, free man, but Christ is all, and in all. (Col 3:4-11)

The life of the righteous fathers and mothers of ancient days, like that of all God's saints, is Christ. God's holy people live for Him alone, for the living God and for His Word. Their reason for being is to praise God, not only in words but in deeds, and so to live.

There is a great difference between *existing* and *living*. Many people exist. Very few really live. Only those who seek God have life. Only those who delight in His commandments and rejoice in accomplishing His will pass beyond mere existence and actually find life. "Seek God, and your soul shall live" (Ps 69:32, LXX).[3] This is the cry of the psalmist David who is especially hymned on this Sunday and on the Sunday after Christmas. His exhortation is in perfect harmony with the words of God given to Moses in His revelation of the divine Law.

"See, I have set before you this day life and good, death and evil. If you obey the commandments of the Lord your God which I command you this day, by loving the Lord your God, by walking in His ways, and by keeping His commandments and His statutes and His ordinances, then you shall live and multiply, and the Lord your God will bless you in the land which you are entering to take possession of it. But if your heart turns away, and you will not hear, but are

[3]This is the Septuagint translation of the verse. The RSV says: "You who seek God, let your hearts revive." The Orthodox liturgy traditionally uses the Septuagint in its worship.

drawn away to worship other gods and serve them, I declare to you this day, that you shall perish; you shall not live long in the land which you are going over the Jordan to enter and possess. I call heaven and earth to witness against you this day, that I have set before you life and death, blessing and curse; therefore choose life, that you and your descendants may live, loving the Lord your God, obeying His voice, and cleaving to Him; for that means life to you and length of days, that you may dwell in the land which the Lord swore to your fathers, to Abraham, to Isaac, and to Jacob, to give them." (Deut 30:15-20)

The holy forefathers and mothers, together with all their descendants, have chosen life. They find it in God's Messiah, Jesus Christ, who is Life itself, God's incarnate Word. The celebration of the Winter Pascha is a celebration of Life in God's Word. For "Christ who is our life" has already appeared (Col 3:4). We have "beheld His glory" (Jn 1:14). Now that glory is hidden in the "form of a slave" (Phil 2:7), but it will be revealed at the end of the ages in power for those who "have loved his appearing" and "live in Him" (2 Tim 4:8; Col 2:6).

You shone as heaven's lights upon the earth,
Enkindling the light of piety.
You called forth the choir of all creation
As you sang to the Master who saves all from temptation,
"Bless Him, O children! Exalt Him, O priests!
Praise Christ, all people, throughout all the ages!"

The Word of the Father comes forth from the Virgin
And without change [to His divinity]
Is born in a cave for my sake.
Let all creation dance with joy
And magnify His all-holy condescension and compassion
    with thanksgiving.[4]

---

[4]Matins of the Sunday of the Holy Forefathers.

15

The Sunday Before Christmas

The Sunday before the feast of Christ's Nativity is again a special day in Orthodox liturgical worship. Once more the Church celebrates the memory of the men and women who believed in the true God and prepared for the coming of His Son and Word in human flesh. The day is a celebration of their faith and an affirmation that it has found its perfection and fulfillment in God's promised Savior who is Jesus Christ the Lord.

Lift up your voice, O Zion, holy city of God,
Proclaim the divine memory of the Fathers.
With Abraham, Isaac, and Jacob
Honor one whose memory is eternal:
For behold, with Judah and Levi we magnify Moses
    the Great,
And with him the wonder-working Aaron.
With David we celebrate the memory of Joshua and
    Samuel,
Calling all with divine songs and praise
To the prefeast of Christ's Nativity,
Praying that we may receive His goodness,
For it is He who grants the world great mercy.

Come, O Elijah,
Who in days of old ascended in the divine chariot of fire.
And divinely-wise Elisha,
Rejoice together with Ezekiel and Josiah.
O honored company of the twelve prophets inspired
    by God,

Exchange glad tidings with them on the birth of the
    Savior.
Sing hymns, all you righteous ones.
O Holy Children who quenched the flames of the
    fire with the dew of the Spirit,
Pray for us, pleading with Christ
That He may grant our souls great mercy.

The Theotokos has been revealed on the earth in truth,
Proclaimed of old by the words of the prophets,
Foretold by the wise patriarchs and the company
    of the righteous.
She will exchange glad tidings with the honor of women:
Sarah, Rebecca, and glorious Hannah,
And Miriam, the sister of Moses.
All the ends of the earth shall rejoice with them,
Together with all of creation.
For God shall come to be born in the flesh,
Granting the world great mercy.

The whole of the Mosaic teachings
Manifested in truth the divine birth of Christ in the flesh
To all who heard the preaching of grace which
    preceded the Law,
Transcending the Law by faith.
And so, since Your nativity brought salvation from
    corruption,
They foretold Your resurrecting of the souls imprisoned
    in death.
O Lord, glory to You![1]

The epistle reading at this Sunday's liturgy is taken from
the letter to the Hebrews, where the faith of those who came
before Christ is noted and praised.

Now faith is the assurance of things hoped for, the
conviction of things not seen. For by it the men of old

[1]Matins of the Sunday before the Nativity.

received divine approval. By faith we understand that the world was created by the word of God, so that what is seen was made out of things which do not appear. . . . And without faith it is impossible to please Him. For whoever would draw near to God must believe that He exists and that He rewards those who seek Him. (Heb 11:1-3, 6)

The letter to the Hebrews lists those who sought the Lord, and demonstrates that their actions were inspired by their faith. By faith Abel . . . By faith Enoch . . . By faith Noah . . . By faith Abraham . . By faith Sarah . . . By faith Isaac . . . By faith Jacob . . . By faith Moses . . . By faith the people . . . By faith Rahab . . . (see Heb 11). The letter tells the story of their faith, insisting that "these all died in faith, not having received what was promised, but having seen it and greeted it from afar" (Heb 11:13). Therefore "God is not ashamed to be called their God, for He has prepared for them a city" (Heb 11:16). This is "the city of the living God, the heavenly Jerusalem" (Heb 12:22) which is given to them by the Messiah-Christ so that their perfection would come together with our own, and all those who have known and believed in His Coming.

And what more shall I say? For time would fail me to tell of Gideon, Barak, Samson, Jephthah, of David and Samuel and the prophets—who through faith conquered kingdoms, enforced justice, received promises, stopped the mouths of lions, quenched raging fire, escaped the edge of the sword, won strength out of weakness, became mighty in war, put foreign armies to flight. Women received their dead by resurrection. Some were tortured, refusing to accept release, that they might rise again to a better life. Others suffered mocking and scourging, and even chains and imprisonment. They were stoned, they were sawn in two, they were killed with the sword; they went about in skins of sheep and goats, destitute, afflicted, ill-treated—of whom the world was not worthy—wandering over

deserts and mountains, and in dens and caves of the
earth. And all these, though well attested by their
faith, did not receive what was promised, since God
had foreseen something better for us, that apart from
us they should not be made perfect. (Heb 11:32-40)

It is an amazing teaching. Those who did such wonderful
things, who had such strength and power, who endured such
afflictions and sufferings, "of whom the world was not
worthy," were nevertheless not made perfect apart from us,
despite the greatness of their faith. For their faith was in the
One who has acted in our time in fulfillment of the promises
first made to them, and then through them to us, their
spiritual children. Since this is so, we must imitate their faith,
acquire their courage, and embody their power, so that we
can in turn become the inheritors of their blessings. This is
the crucial message of the Sunday dedicated to their memory.

Therefore, since we are surrounded by so great a cloud
of witnesses, let us also lay aside every weight, and
sin which clings so closely, and let us run with per-
severance the race that is set before us, looking to
Jesus the pioneer and perfecter of our faith, who for
the joy that was set before Him endured the cross,
despising the shame, and is seated at the right hand
of the throne of God. (Heb 12:1-2)

The Virgin now comes to Bethlehem to give birth to Christ
Who has become an infant in the flesh.
Christ has voluntarily become poor.
Christ has become visible.
Let heaven and earth greatly rejoice!

Skip, O hills and mountains!
Dance, O prophets who spoke of God!
Clap your hands, O peoples and nations!
The Salvation and Enlightenment of all draws near.
He comes to be born in the city of Bethlehem.

The Rich One becomes poor,
Making poor those who have grown rich in evil.
God is revealed as a mortal man,
Born without change [to His divinity] of a Maiden
    who has not known a man.
Let us all praise Him in song
For He has been glorified![2]

---

[2]Matins of the Sunday before the Nativity.

16

The Genealogy of Jesus Christ

The gospel reading for the divine liturgy on the Sunday before Christmas is "the genealogy of Jesus Christ, the son of David, the son of Abraham," taken from the gospel according to Saint Matthew.[1] This genealogy lists the generations of people from Abraham to David, to the Babylonian captivity of the people of Israel, to the birth of Jesus. It is a selected genealogy, ending in the appearance of "Joseph, the husband of Mary, of whom Jesus was born, who is called Christ" (Mt 1:16). It differs from the genealogy presented in Saint Luke's gospel which begins with Jesus "being the son (as was supposed) of Joseph," and goes back all the way not simply to Abraham but to Adam (Lk 3:23-38).

There are many purposes for presenting the genealogy of Jesus in the gospels, chief among which is the affirmation that Jesus, being in truth the Son of God, as all the gospels testify, has come "in the flesh" as a real human being. This affirmation was critically important in the time of the apostles and the first Christian generations because, unlike today, the temptation of the early period of Christianity was not to deny Jesus' divinity, but to deny His real and authentic humanity.

As a matter of historical fact, the first Christian heretics were those who said that Jesus was some sort of divine being (how this was explained had many variations and versions) who only appeared to be a true man, but was not really one since "flesh and blood" were taken to be intrinsically degrading if not downright evil. Thus the apostle Paul had to insist that in Jesus, who belongs to the Jews "according to the

[1]The gospel reading for the liturgy is Mt 1:1-25.

flesh" (Rom 9:5), the "whole fulness of deity dwells *bodily*" (Col 2:9), and that it is the same Jesus who died and was buried and raised in the flesh as a real man, who is Messiah and Lord.[2]

The letter to the Hebrews is even more emphatic about the real humanity of Jesus than are the epistles of the apostle Paul already referred to. This letter insists that Jesus is not an angel or some other sort of celestial spirit, but is the Son of God Himself (Heb 1-2). It insists with equal, if not greater power and pathos, however, that this Son of God was made for a while "lower than the angels," that being a real human being, "by the grace of God He might taste death for every one" (Heb 2:9).

> Since therefore the children share in flesh and blood, He Himself likewise partook of the same nature, that through death He might destroy him who has the power of death, that is, the devil, and deliver all those who through fear of death were subject to lifelong bondage. For surely it is not with angels that He is concerned but with the descendants of Abraham. Therefore He had to be made like His brethren in every respect, so that He might become a merciful and faithful high priest in the service of God, to make expiation for the sins of the people. For because He Himself has suffered and been tempted, He is able to help those who are tempted. (Heb 2:14-18)

> In the days of His flesh, Jesus offered up prayers and supplications, with loud cries and tears, to Him who was able to save Him from death, and He was heard for His godly fear. Although He was a Son, He learned obedience through what He suffered; and being made perfect He became the source of eternal salvation to all who obey Him ... (Heb 5:7-9)

The letters of Saint John are the most powerful of all the New Testament scriptures on this point. It seems that the

[2]See 1 Cor 15:3-4; Gal 4:4; Phil 2:6-11.

apostle and his community were plagued with people who refused to acknowledge the real incarnation of the Son of God as an authentic human being. The beloved disciple of the Lord soundly condemns them with a violence of conviction that would be shocking to many Christians today.

> Beloved, do not believe every spirit, but test the spirits to see whether they are of God; for many false prophets have gone out into the world. By this you know the Spirit of God: every spirit which confesses that Jesus Christ has come in the flesh is of God, and every spirit which does not confess Jesus is not of God. This is the spirit of antichrist, of which you heard that it was coming, and now it is in the world already. (1 Jn 4:1-3)

> For many deceivers have gone out into the world, men who will not acknowledge the coming of Jesus Christ in the flesh; such a one is the deceiver and the antichrist. Look to yourselves, that you may not lose what you have worked for, but may win a full reward. Any one who goes ahead and does not abide in the doctrine of Christ does not have God; he who abides in the doctrine has both the Father and the Son. If any one comes to you and does not bring this doctrine, do not receive him into the house or give him any greeting; for he who greets him shares his wicked work. (2 Jn 7-11)

Another reason for the genealogies of Jesus in the gospels is to demonstrate that the Lord is indeed the fulfillment of the promise made to Abraham, affirmed, for example, in the song of the Virgin Mary in Saint Luke's gospel (Lk 1:55), and defended as a theological truth in the writings of the apostle Paul, for example, in his letter to the Galatians where he says that "the promises were made to Abraham and to his offspring. . . . which is Christ" (Gal 3:16). Their purpose is also to demonstrate that Jesus is equally the fulfillment of the promise to king David that one of his sons will sit upon his throne and reign over God's kingdom which has literally no end.[3]

The genealogies in the gospels of Saints Matthew and Luke are made to and from Joseph. This is not to give the impression that Jesus came from Joseph's seed. Both gospels are absolutely clear on this point. Jesus is born from the Virgin Mary by the power of the Holy Spirit. The point is rather that Joseph is Jesus' father according to the law, and it is from the father that one's lawful descent is to be traced. Jesus' legal father is "Joseph, son of David,"[4] the legal husband of Mary (Mt 1:20).

One other important point is made in listing the human generations which led to the birth of Jesus. This is the fact that God is faithful to His promises even though His chosen people are often not faithful. Among the people from whom Jesus came are both sinners and heathens. In a word, Jesus comes not only from the righteous and holy, but from the wicked and sinful. And He comes not only from Jews, but from Gentiles. The names of the four women specifically mentioned in Saint Matthew's list—Tamar, Rahab, Ruth, and the wife of Uriah (Bathsheba)—were noted, not to say notorious, Gentiles, including one of David's own wives, the mother of Solomon. The point to be seen here is one beautifully made in an early Christian hymn quoted in the Bible in the second letter to Timothy:

> If we have died with Him,
>   we shall also live with Him;
> If we endure,
>   we shall also reign with Him;
> If we deny Him,
>   He also will deny us;
> If we are faithless,
>   He remains faithful—for He cannot deny Himself.
> (2 Tim 2:11-13)

[3]See Ps 89; Lk 1:32, 69; Heb 1.
[4]See also Lk 1:27; 2:4. The Church teaches in her songs and hymns that Mary is also from the house and lineage of David, though this would have no significance in establishing Jesus' claims as the Anointed One, the promised Messiah.

This is the wonderful witness of the genealogies of Jesus: If we are faithless, the Lord God remains faithful—for He cannot deny Himself!

> Behold, the time of our salvation is at hand.
> Prepare yourself, O cavern,
> For the Virgin approaches to give birth to her Son.
> Be glad and rejoice, O Bethlehem, land of Judah,
> For from you our Lord shines forth as the dawn.
> Give ear, you mountains and hills
> And all lands surrounding Judea,
> For Christ is coming to save the people
> Whom He has created and whom He loves.[5]

---

[5]Vespers of the Sunday before the Nativity.

17

Let Us Celebrate, O People!

The prefeast celebration of the Lord's Nativity begins in earnest five days before Christmas.[1] The services of each of these days call the faithful to prepare themselves for the festival, and to prepare the festival itself.

Let us celebrate, O people,
The prefeast of Christ's Nativity!
Let us raise our minds on high,
Going up in spirit to Bethlehem.
With the eyes of our souls let us behold the Virgin
As she hastens to the cave to give birth to the Lord and
    God of all.
When Joseph first saw the mighty wonder
He thought that he saw only a human child wrapped in
    swaddling clothes,
But from all that came to pass he discovered the Child
    to be the true God
Who grants great mercy to the world.

Let us celebrate, O people,
The prefeast of Christ's Nativity!
Let us raise our minds on high,
Going up in spirit to Bethlehem.
Let us behold the great mystery in the cavern,
For Eden is opened once again
When God comes forth from a pure Virgin,

[1]In some parish churches these services are spread out throughout the lenten season (e.g., one being done each week), so that those who cannot come to church every day the week before Christmas may experience them.

Remaining the same perfect God and becoming perfect
   man.
Therefore let us cry out to Him:
Holy God, Father without beginning!
Holy Mighty, Incarnate Son!
Holy Immortal, the Spirit and Comforter!
O Holy Trinity, glory to You![2]

Let us celebrate, O people! Let us go up in spirit! Let us
raise our minds on high! These are not simply exclamations
of enthusiastic piety and emotional devotion for the few
strange people who like that sort of thing. They are exhorta-
tions and commands which are essential to the spiritual life
of all human beings who must hear and obey as if their life
depended upon it. Because, in a real sense, it does.

We are created to celebrate the gifts of God, and God
Himself. This is our reason for being. It is the substance of
our lives. All human sin, including the "original sin" of Adam
and Eve, is a failure to celebrate properly who God is and
what He does for the sake of those who are made in His
image and likeness.

The sinful celebration, which ultimately is no celebration
at all but simply sin, is one which excludes God and attempts
to rejoice in something other than Him and His presence and
action in the world. In other words, it is the celebration of
God's gifts without reference to God the Giver. And its
inevitable result, necessarily and organically, is dissatisfaction,
distress, depression, and finally death itself.

The Christmas season is a time of celebration, a season of
gladness and joy. But many people, including many who consider themselves Christians, are devoid of the joyful spirit of
celebration. They find the season irritating and unfulfilling,
disappointing and depressing, even admitting at times that
they are glad when it is over! The obvious reason for this is
that they are celebrating wrongly.

Some people do not celebrate God and His gifts, including the gift of Jesus Christ, at all. They celebrate carnal pleasures and fleshly lusts. They may have a lot of fun, but

[2]Vespers of the first day of the prefeast of Christmas, December 20.

authentic joy eludes them. They come to the end of the "holiday season" completely burnt out, while craving more of the same because what they got, whatever is was, was certainly not enough. And, in any case, it's now over and gone.

Others come to the festal season with the firm intention to celebrate God's gift of the Savior. They are super-serious. They clench their fists and grit their teeth, determined to keep it "religious" and "spiritual." But when the season is over they are left empty and dead because they have spent their energies looking at others, condemning their foolish behavior, and becoming miserable because of it. Such people are those who instead of filling the human joys of the season with the divine grace of the Lord, ruin the holy time for themselves and their families and friends by cursing the "secularism" and "commercialism" which has infected the feast, instead of blessing God and enjoying the festival for what it really is. While berating their fellows for not "keeping Christ in Christmas," they have actually excluded Him from their own celebration by their Pharisaic self-righteousness and condemnation of their brothers and sisters for whom Christ has come and for whom He has died, whether they know it or not.

Let us celebrate, O people! But let us celebrate properly. Let us go up to Bethlehem, and not into the houses of others. Let us lift up our minds to the Lord, and not let them stray into the lives of our neighbors. Let us concentrate on God and rejoice in His mercy and love for the world, even the "secularized" and "commercialized" world where the devil reigns. Let us not ruin the festival for ourselves and for our loved ones because of what others are doing or not doing. Let us strive to "keep Christ in Christmas" for ourselves first of all, by keeping Christ in ourselves and ourselves in Christ. Then Christmas will be the God-given celebration which it is, the celebration of God's Coming in the person of His Son. Only in this way will our celebration be pleasing to the Lord, fulfilling for ourselves, and inspiring for others. For it will then be a living testimony to what a celebration really is when it is what God made it to be.

The world today urgently needs divine celebration. And so do many Christians and Christian churches. For while some are having fun, and others are condemning them for doing so, neither the one nor the other is really joyful and at peace. For no one can be satisfied without the presence of the merciful God who loves His creatures and comes to heal and forgive them their foolishness and sin. And no celebration is truly satisfying without God's compassionate presence of love.

Come, O faithful,
Begin the celebration!
Sing with the wise men and shepherds!
Salvation comes from the Virgin's womb,
Recalling the faithful to life.[3]

Let us reject the corruption of passions,
Awaiting the visitation of Christ.
Let us come to our senses and receive knowledge,
The gift of the undefiled Lord
Who comes to be clothed in our flesh,
Refashioning us in godliness.

Beholding Christ, let us be exalted through humility.
Let us abandon earthly passions with zeal for good.
Let us learn through faith not to be proud of heart.
Let us humiliate ourselves in spirit,
That by good deeds we may exalt Him who comes to
    be born.[4]

[3]Vespers of the first day of the prefeast of Christmas.
[4]Compline of the first day of the prefeast of Christmas.

18

Christ Comes to Restore the Image

Human beings, male and female, are made in the image and according to the likeness of God.[1] This is a fundamental doctrine of the Judeo-Christian worldview. It means that we humans are not simply the product of our heredity and environment, of our biological makeup and genetic construction. Neither are we simply the result of some accidental combination of physical particles and material cells, nor merely the outcome of historical processes, economic systems, and sociological configurations. Our lives do not consist in the amount of our possessions, our will to power, our educational opportunities, or our sexual drives and satisfactions. All of these, and many other factors are important in peoples' lives, even critical, but they are not what make us human. We human beings are *human* because our fundamental and essential property is to be the most perfect created expressions of God's being and life. We are made to be "imitators of God" and "partakers of the divine nature" (Eph 5:1; 2 Pet 1:4).

To be made in the image and likeness of God is to be both a spiritual and material being. It is to be personal, free, self-determining, and self-aware. It is to be able to know and to do good, to be able to act and to care. It is to be capable of governing and cultivating, creating and ruling. It is, in a word, as all of the Orthodox Christian saints have taught, to be able to be by God's grace and good will absolutely *everything* that God Himself is by nature.

God is a living God, and we are made also to live. God is good, and we are made to be good. God is wise, and we are

[1]See Gen 1:26-27; 5:1-2.

made to be wise. God is peaceful and joyful, kind and compassionate, powerful and gentle—and that is the way that we
too are to be. God lives forever and never dies, and we also
are made to be immortal. God governs all that He has made,
and we, the creatures made in His image and likeness, are
made to care for His creation. We can carry the connections
on endlessly; they apply in every case. Whatever God is, we
are made by Him to become. And most important of all, and
that which contains all specific and particular elements: *God
is Love* (1 Jn 4:8, 16). And we His creatures are made by
Him also to be Love. We are made to love as He loves. To
love all things which He loves. And to love Him first of all.

The cause of all sadness and sorrow is that human beings
have failed to be—and therefore endlessly to become—what
God has made them to be. In the ultimate sense, they have
failed to love. This is the meaning of the sin of Adam and
Eve in the Bible. Human beings use their godlike natures and
employ their godlike energies for evil instead of good, for lies
instead of truth, for destruction instead of creation, for death
instead of life. They corrupt their being, distorting the divine
image within them and losing their likeness to God.[2]

Orthodox Christians affirm that Jesus Christ has come to
restore God's image and likeness in human beings. He
enabled them to be what they were created to be in the
beginning. Jesus does this, not simply because He is God's
only-begotten Son and Word, but because He is also "the
image of the invisible God" (Col 1:15; 2 Cor 4:4).[3] Those
who see Jesus, as He Himself has said, see God the Father.

[2]Some Orthodox writers, including some of the Church fathers like Saint
Gregory of Nyssa and Saint Maximus the Confessor, make a distinction between
image and *likeness*. They say that God's image in man is what is given and
can never be destroyed, and that God's likeness in man is what must be
nurtured and developed, or else it will be lost. This distinction is not always
followed. Some Church fathers, like Saint Athanasius the Great, do not make
it, but use image and likeness synonymously. The Church's liturgy tends to
follow the biblical and Athanasian practice and does not make a fine distinction between the two terms. Whatever the use of terms, however, it should
be noted that the substantial teaching is the same.

[3]In the RSV translation of the Bible, Col 1:15 reads, "He [the beloved
Son] is the *image* of the invisible God; and 2 Cor 4:4 reads, "Christ, who is
the *likeness* of God." In both cases in Greek, however, the word for image
and likeness is the same: *eikon,* from which we get the English word "icon."

Philip said to Him, "Lord, show us the Father, and we shall be satisfied." Jesus said to him, "Have I been with you so long, and yet you do not know me, Philip? He who has seen me has seen the Father; how can you say, 'Show us the Father'?" (Jn 14:8-9)

Christ restores the image of God in human beings, being Himself God's uncreated and eternal image, by becoming a real human being, the "last" and "final" Adam, the "man from heaven."

Thus it is written, "The first man Adam became a living being"; the last Adam became a life-giving spirit. But it is not the spiritual which is first but the physical, and then the spiritual. The first man was from the earth, a man of dust; the second man is from heaven. As was the man of dust, so are those who are of the dust; and as is the man of heaven, so are those who are of heaven. Just as we have borne the image of the man of dust, we shall also bear the image of the man of heaven. (1 Cor 15:45-49)

As the second and final Adam, Jesus does everything that the first and original Adam was called—but failed—to do. He obeys God. He honors His Name. He delights in His Presence. He adores His Divinity. He gives thanks for His gifts. He speaks His words. He does His works. He accomplishes His will. And so He fulfills Himself in a human manner as one made in God's image and likeness. But being the Son of God Himself, God's uncreated Image and Word, His accomplishment extends to all human beings and is made fully and freely available to all people. "For as in Adam all die, so also in Christ shall all be made alive" (1 Cor 15:22). For Adam himself was but "a type of the One who was to come" (Rom 5:14). This is Jesus.

But the free gift is not like the trespass. For if many died through one man's trespass, much more have the grace of God and the free gift in the grace of that one

man Jesus Christ abounded for many. And the free
gift is not like the effect of that one man's sin. For the
judgment following one trespass brought condemnation, but the free gift of righteousness brings life
through the one man Jesus Christ. (Rom 5:15-17)

This is the message of Christmas. There is a new Adam.
There is a restored image of God. It is the restored image of
the Image Himself, God's Son and Word, Jesus Christ. In
Him humankind has found its fulfillment and perfection. In
Him human beings can live. In Him all people can complete
themselves as creatures made to be by God's grace all that
God Himself is by nature. In Him all people can be *human.*

Prepare, O Bethlehem,
For Eden has been opened to all.
Adorn yourself, O Ephratha,
For the Tree of Life blossoms forth from the Virgin in
the cave.
Her womb is a spiritual paradise planted with the fruit
divine;
If we eat of it, we shall live forever and not die like Adam.
Christ is coming to restore the image which He made in the
beginning.[4]

The Creator, the Wisdom of God, draws near,
The mist of the prophets' promise is dispersed.
Joy clears the skies,
Truth is resplendent,
The dark shadows are dispelled,
The gates of Eden are opened,
Adam dances in exultation:
Our Creator and God wills to fashion us anew.[5]

You partook of human flesh, O Christ,
Offspring of the seed of Abraham.

[4]Troparion of the prefeast of the Nativity. Ephratha, often mentioned in
the liturgy of Christmas, is the region in which Bethlehem is located. The
name is used as a synonym for Bethlehem, the city of David. See Mic 5:2.
[5]Matins of the second day of the prefeast of the Nativity, December 21.

You came to give grace upon grace,
Restoring Your image
And freeing us from corruption.
For the Father has sent You, the only-begotten Son,
As atonement for the world.[6]

O Lord my God,
I will sing You a birthday song,
A hymn on the prefeast,
For by Your Nativity You give me a divine rebirth,
And lead me up to my first perfection.[7]

[6]Compline of the third day of the prefeast of the Nativity, December 22.
The expression "grace upon grace" comes from Jn 1:16.
[7]Compline of the eve of the Nativity.

19

The Tree of Life Blossoms

In the hymns for the prefeast of Christ's Nativity, Jesus' birth heralds a return to paradise. The Messiah is born and the gates of Eden are opened. The Savior comes and the tree of life blossoms.

The prophecy of all the prophets is fulfilled,
Christ is born in Bethlehem.
Paradise is opened to those of Adam's race.[1]

Prepare, O Bethlehem,
For Eden has been opened to all.
Adorn yourself, O Ephratha,
For the Tree of Life blossoms forth from the Virgin
    in the cave.
Her womb is a spiritual paradise planted with the
    fruit divine;
If we eat of it, we shall live forever and not die like Adam.
Christ is coming to restore the image which He made
    in the beginning.[2]

Paradise is not a place on the map. It is a condition of spirit. When a person knows God and lives in communion with Him, this is paradise. When a person does not know God and lives in communion with his own nothingness, this is death and hell, the "land of forgetfulness" (Ps 88:11-12). Only the person who knows God really lives. Jesus Himself

[1]Matins of the second day of the prefeast of the Nativity, December 21.
[2]Troparion of the prefeast of the Nativity.

says so: "And this is eternal life, that they know Thee, the only true God, and Jesus Christ whom Thou hast sent" (Jn 17:3).

The biblical story of paradise says that in the garden of Eden two trees were growing that had particular significance. One was the "tree of the knowledge of good and evil," the other was the "tree of life." In the scriptural story, the Lord tells Adam and Eve that they may eat the fruit of all the trees of the garden except that of the tree of the knowledge of good and evil. They were told that if they partook of the fruit of that tree, if they even touched it, they would surely die. God did not say that He would kill them. He said that the act itself would kill them, like a participation in poison.[3]

In the Church tradition there are many interpretations of this eating of the tree of the knowledge of good and evil. Although all interpretations agree that the act was destructive for us, and that it was committed through disobedience, mistrust, pride, lack of gratitude, and, ultimately, lack of love for God on the part of His creatures, there is a variety of understandings about the act itself.

Saint Gregory Nazianzen, for example, thinks that the communion with the tree symbolized an advanced state of spiritual union with God for which Adam and Eve were not ready. He thought that God would ultimately have let them partake of the tree when they were sufficiently mature. Their sin, therefore, was one of presumption. The idea is that we have to grow up in our relationship with God. We have to mature and develop. We have to achieve illumination, contemplation, and union with God through a long spiritual process. We cannot jump into it before we are ready. If we do, it destroys us.[4]

Father Alexander Schmemann had another idea about the meaning of Adam and Eve's eating of the tree of the knowledge of good and evil.

Man ate the forbidden fruit. The fruit of that one tree,

---

[3]See Gen 2:15-3:7.
[4]See Gregory Nazianzen, Oration 39, *On the Holy Lights or Epiphany,* 7; Oration 45, *Second Homily on Pascha,* 8.

whatever else it may signify, was unlike every other fruit in the Garden: it was not offered as a gift to man. Not given, not blessed by God, it was food whose eating was condemned to be communion with itself alone, and not with God. It is the image of the world loved for itself, and eating it is the image of life understood as an end in itself.[5]

Most interpretations of the story, however, simply say that Adam's sin was the actual experience of evil, the act of breaking relationship with God, of coming to know the difference between good and evil by the realization of wickedness. It does not matter what the deed was, in this understanding. The story is not about one or another specific transgression. It is about transgression itself. It shows what happens when human beings commit any kind of evil, any kind of sin, any kind of transgression or infraction of the will of God.

God's placing of the tree of the knowledge of good and evil in the midst of the garden is not done as some sort of ethical or spiritual test. It is not an "exam." It is an inevitable reality. The possibility of sin always stands in the midst of the garden. It has to be there. It cannot be otherwise. We are free. God therefore tells us: The tree is there. Don't taste it, don't even touch it. But it was seen to be "good for food" and "a delight to the eyes," and "was to be desired to make one wise."[6] And Adam and Eve could not resist. They partook. And they died.

But there is also in the midst of the garden another tree, the "tree of life." This symbolizes for all churchly interpreters the actualization of communion with God; of obedience, of truth, of life itself. It is the image of what the New Testament writers call the "kingdom of God" which, in the teaching of the apostle Paul, "is not food and drink but righteousness and peace and joy in the Holy Spirit" (Rom 14:17). And the fruit of this tree, which is the fruit of the Holy Spirit, the Spirit of Truth, is "love, joy, peace, patience, kindness, goodness faithfulness, gentleness, self-control" (Gal 5:22-23). It

[5]Father Alexander Schmemann, *For the Life of the World*, p. 16.
[6]See Gen 3:6.

is the knowledge of God by actual experience. It is wisdom and understanding. It is clarity and insight. It is the knowledge of good but not of evil. For knowledge in the biblical sense always means *experience*: tasting and touching, communing and partaking.[7]

> Happy is the man who finds wisdom,
>   and the man who gets understanding . . .
> Her ways are ways of pleasantness,
>   and all her paths are peace.
> She is a tree of life to those who lay hold of her;
>   those who hold her fast are called happy.
>   (Prov 3:13, 17-18)
> The fruit of the righteous is a tree of life,
>   but lawlessness takes away lives. (Prov 11:30)

When Christ is born the tree of life is planted on earth. It blossoms forth from a virgin in a cavern. Her womb becomes a spiritual paradise. And all the mortal children of Adam and Eve are invited to come and eat of its fruit, the fruit of the Spirit given by Jesus. And they partake of the eternal life which He brings. This is what God's Spirit says to the churches: "To him who conquers [over the devil with Jesus, the new Adam] I will grant to eat of the tree of life, which is in the paradise of God" (Rev 2:7). This is Jesus' own promise in the same book of Revelation:

> "Behold, I am coming soon, bringing My recompense, to repay every one for what he has done. I am the Alpha and the Omega, the first and the last, the beginning and the end."
>   Blessed are those who wash their robes, that they may have the right to the tree of life and that they may enter the city by the gates. Outside are the mur-

---

[7]The word for *knowledge* in the Bible is used for the sexual intercourse between man and woman; e.g., "Now Adam *knew* Eve his wife, and she conceived" (Gen 4:1). This indicates the experiential and communal understanding of knowledge which is anything but abstract or theoretical.

derers and idolaters, and every one who loves and practices falsehood.

"I Jesus have sent My angel to you with this testimony for the churches. I am the root and the offspring of David, the bright morning star." (Rev 22:12-16)

The root and offspring of David is born. The bright morning star has appeared. Christ has come, and the tree of life blossoms for all to partake.

Make ready, O Bethlehem, for Eden is opened.
Prepare, O Ephratha, for Adam and Eve are renewed.
Salvation enters the world and the curse is destroyed.
Make ready, O hearts of righteous men,
Instead of myrrh, bring songs as an offering of wisdom.
Receive salvation and immortality for your bodies and
    souls.
Behold, the Master who lays in a manger urges us to
    complete our spiritual songs.
Let us cry to Him without ceasing: O Lord, glory to You![8]

---

[8]Vespers of the fourth day of the prefeast of the Nativity, December 23.

20

The Two Comings of Christ

In churches of catholic tradition in the Christian West, the Christmas "advent" season greatly emphasizes the second coming of the Lord. The faithful are called in their preparation for Christmas to look beyond the Savior's coming in "the form of a slave . . . the likeness of men" (Phil 2:7), to His coming again in glory at the end of the ages to judge the living and the dead in the Kingdom of God.

In the Eastern Orthodox tradition, the second coming of Christ is liturgically emphasized during the first three days of Holy Week before the springtime Pascha of the Lord's death and resurrection. At the services of these holy days the scripture readings and hymns all refer to the end of the world and the judgment of creation by the victorious Lord who enters His glory by way of the Cross.

During the Christmas prefeast season, the connection between the first coming of God's Son as the Suffering Servant, the Lamb of God who takes upon Himself the sins of the World, and His second coming as the triumphant King and Judge of the universe is not overtly stressed in any of the church services. But it is clearly implied in virtually all of the songs, hymns and lections. The Old Testament prophecies read at the hours, vespers, and matins on the day before the Nativity quite specifically proclaim the messianic age which Jesus is born to bring, but which He will manifest in power only at the end of history. And several verses which are sung during the season directly refer to the interrelationship between the Master's two comings.

Christ our Judge commands us to be vigilant.

We wait expectantly for His visitation,
For He comes to be born of a virgin.

At Your awesome second coming, O Christ,
Number me with the sheep at Your right hand,
For You took up Your abode in the flesh to save us.

At Your first coming to us, O Christ,
You desired to save the race of Adam;
When You come again to judge us,
Show mercy on those who honor Your Holy Nativity.[1]

The Christmas prefeast hymns, especially the canons, consciously refer to the hymns of the services of Holy Week before the springtime Pascha. In many of them, Easter paschal themes are replaced by Winter paschal themes, with just a few words being changed in each verse.[2] Thus, what is effected at these services is a sort of "triple connection." Christ's Nativity, with His Epiphany in the Jordan, is referred to His Passion and Resurrection, which is then refererd to His Coming at the end of the ages. In making this triple connection, the entire Mystery of Christ is placed before the believers for their contemplation and communion.

Jesus was born in order to die. Indeed, of all humans who ever lived on earth, God's Son is the only one who entered the world for this purpose. He came to die so that we might live in and through Him. The eternal life which He brings to the world is already present and active in those who receive Him, but it will be manifested fully and completely in a way which no one can question, doubt, or resist only at the end of the ages. Christians are those who remember and celebrate the fact that God has visited His people in the person of His Son in order to be crucified and raised. And so they are also those who await His Coming, believing that all of God's promises made in and through Jesus will be actualized in the age to come. Therefore they expect nothing

[1] Ode 9 of the canon of compline of the second day of the prefeast of the Nativity, December 21
[2] See above, pp. 10-11.

here. They want nothing here. They know that they will get nothing here. Their Savior's promise for this age is only persecution and tribulation.

> Jesus said, "Truly, I say to you, there is no one who has left house or brothers or sisters or mother or father or children or lands, for My sake and for the gospel, who will not receive a hundredfold now in this time, houses and brothers and sisters and mothers and children and lands, with persecutions, and in the age to come eternal life." (Mk 10:29-30)

> "If the world hates you, know that it has hated Me before it hated you. If you were of the world, the world would love its own; but because you are not of the world, but I chose you out of the world, therefore the world hates you. Remember the word that I said to you, 'A servant is not greater than his master.' If they persecuted Me, they will persecute you; if they kept My word, they will keep yours also." (Jn 15:18-20)

> "The hours is coming, indeed it has come, when you will be scattered, every man to his home, and will leave Me alone; yet I am not alone, for the Father is with Me. I have said this to you, that in Me you may have peace. In the world you have tribulation; but be of good cheer, I have overcome the world." (Jn 16-33)

Christians live between the two comings of Christ. They remember His first coming to be sacrificed. They anticipate His second coming to reign. This is vividly portrayed in traditional Orthodox church buildings where the "royal gates" of the icon screen in front of the altar table are flanked by the icons of the Theotokos and Child on the one side, and the Lord Jesus in glory on the other. To the uninitiated it may seem as though these are simply pictures of Mary and Jesus put on the same level. This is not so. The icons which frame the Orthodox altar are images of the two comings of Christ.

Mary is not alone in her icon; she is holding the Christ Child, who is not shown as a baby, but as the Son of God incarnate "in the form of a slave . . . in the likeness of men" (Phil 2:7). This is the icon of Christ's first coming. And the icon on the right of the doors is not a picture of Jesus as He was on the earth. It is His image in glory as King and Lord, the icon of His second coming.

The two comings of Christ are held together in Christian thought, action, and prayer at all times. They cannot be separated. When they are, it is the end of Christian faith, life and worship. The first coming without the second is a meaningless tragedy. The second coming without the first is an absurd impossibility. Jesus is born to bring God's kingdom. He dies to prove His kingship. He rises to establish His reign. He comes again in glory to share it with His people. In the kingdom of God there are no subjects. All rule with the risen Messiah. He came, and is coming, for this purpose alone.

> You have taken me captive with longing for You,
>   O Christ,
> And have transformed me with Your divine love.
> Burn up my sins with the fire of Your Spirit
> And count me worthy to take my fill of delight in You
> That dancing with joy, I may magnify Your two Comings.[3]

---

[3]This is a pre-Communion prayer in some Orthodox prayer books (e.g., see *A Manual of Eastern Orthodox Prayers* [London: SPCK, 1945] p. 77 [republished in 1984 by Saint Vladimir's Seminary Press, Crestwood, New York]). It was written by Saint John of Damascus and is originally found in the second canon for matins of the feast of the Transfiguration, August 6, ode 9, troparion 3.

21

Let Us Enjoy the Master's Hospitality

One of the beloved songs of Orthodox Christians is sung on Holy Thursday before the springtime Pascha of the Lord. It is the last ode of the matins' canon which is also sung in place of the Hymn to the Theotokos at the celebration of the Eucharist which on that day specifically commemorates the Mystical Supper of the Lord. This very same song is sung as the last ode of the compline canon on the third day of the prefeast of Christmas.

Come, O faithful,
Let us enjoy the Master's hospitality,
The banquet of immortality.
In the upper chamber with uplifted minds
Let us receive the exalted words of the Word
Whom we magnify.

The troparia which follow the singing of this ode are exactly those of the Holy Thursday commemoration of the Lord's Mystical Supper with, once again, just a few of the words changed to fit the Nativity celebration.

After meeting the chief priests,
Herod the deceiver spoke to the wise men:
Go and search for the Child.
Declare quickly to me when you find Him.
But You destroyed his plot, O Lord,
Putting to shame the lawless slave of evil.

He who is the Fashioner of all,

94

Begotten of the Father before all ages,
Comes to be born of the Virgin.
He is the Wisdom, Word, and Power of God.
We magnify Him as God and man, the Lord,
Brought forth in two natures yet being one Person.
I am revealed as a man in essence and not imagination
    [says the Lord];
By this communion human nature is united to Me and
    made godlike.
Know that I am Your Savior,
Who proceeds from the Virgin's womb,
Whom blessing in faith we magnify in song.[1]

Like virtually every song and hymn of the season, these
verses clearly state who Jesus Christ is and why He has come.
He is the eternal Son of God; God's uncreated Wisdom,
Word, and Power.[2] He is the Fashioner of all, the One by
whom, in whom, and for whom all things are made.[3] He
becomes man without change to His divinity. Remaining God,
for indeed, it is impossible for Him to cease being divine,
He becomes a human being: Jesus of Nazareth. He is, therefore, as it came to be formulated over centuries of painful
and bitter controversy, "one Person in two natures."

As God's only-begotten Son, Jesus Christ is a divine person
with the divine nature of God the Father Himself. And he
becomes, as the song says, a real human being "in essence
and not in imagination."[4] Thus He is, according to the dogmatic definition of the Council of Chalcedon, now known by
the Orthodox as the fourth ecumenical council, really God
and really man. There is no separation or division whatsoever
between His divinity and His humanity. And yet there is no
mingling of the two radically different "natures," and no
change to either of them in what they essentially are. In a

---

[1]Compline of the third day of the prefeast of the Nativity, December 22.
[2]See Jn 1:1; 1 Cor 1:24.
[3]See Jn 1:2-3; Heb 1:2-3; 1 Cor 8:6; Col 1:15-20.
[4]This sentence recalls the false teaching of some early Christians that
Jesus only appeared to be human but was not really so, called *docetism* from
the Greek word "to seem" or "to appear." In the text the word "imagination"
is *phantasia*, fantasy, i.e., not substantial reality.

word, He is *divine* with exactly the same divinity as God the
Father and the Holy Spirit. And He is *human* with exactly
the same humanity as that of every human being who has ever
lived or will live.[5]

A wonderful way of stating the reason why God sent His
Son into the world as a man is simply to say that He came
that we might "enjoy the Master's hospitality" by partaking
of the "banquet of immortality." The Lord appeared on earth
to "set a table" in the wilderness of this world in order to
feed us with the living Bread, the Bread which comes down
from heaven, the Bread of Life which He Himself is. He
came to feed us with His own Body and Blood.

> Jesus said to them, "I am the bread of life; he who
> comes to Me shall not hunger, and he who believes in
> Me shall never thirst. But I said to you that you have
> seen Me and yet do not believe. All that the Father
> gives Me will come to Me; and him who comes to Me
> I will not cast out. For I have come down from heaven,
> not to do My own will, but the will of Him who sent
> Me; and this is the will of Him who sent Me, that I
> should lose nothing of all that He has given Me, but
> raise it up the last day. For this is the will of My
> Father, that every one who sees the Son and believes
> in Him should have eternal life; and I will raise him
> up at the last day." . . .
>
> "I am the living bread which came down from
> heaven; if any one eats of this bread, he will live for
> ever; and the bread which I shall give for the life
> of the world is My flesh." . . .

[5]The definition of the Council of Chalcedon says that Jesus Christ is
"perfect God and perfect man," being "of one essence with God in regard to
His divinity" and "of one essence with humans in regard to His humanity."
It describes the "union" between divinity and humanity in Jesus as "hypo-
static," i.e., in the one "hypostasis" or "person" of the Son of God. And it
defines how this "union" occurs by the use of four negative adverbs: *indi-
visibly, inseparably, immutably,* and *unconfusedly.* For the text of this con-
ciliar definition and a further explanation of it, see Thomas Hopko, *The
Orthodox Faith: An Elementary Handbook,* vol. 1: *Doctrine* (New York:
Department of Religious Education, Orthodox Church in America, 1976,
revised edition) pp. 77-79.

So Jesus said to them, "Truly, truly, I say to you, unless you eat the flesh of the Son of man and drink His blood, you have no life in you; he who eats My flesh and drinks My blood has eternal life, and I will raise him up at the last day. For My flesh is food indeed, and My blood is drink indeed. He who eats My flesh and drinks My blood abides in Me, and I in him. As the living Father sent Me, and I live because of the Father, so he who eats Me will live because of Me. This is the bread which came down from heaven, not such as the fathers ate and died; he who eats this bread will live for ever." (Jn 6:35-40, 51, 53-58)

The kingdom of God which the Messiah brings is described in the Bible as a banquet. Jesus Himself compares God's kingdom in several of His parables to a festive supper.[6] He tells His disciples at the final paschal meal that they will sit at table, eating and drinking in the kingdom of God.

"You are those who have continued with Me in My trials; and I assign to you, as My Father assigned to Me, a kingdom, that you may eat and drink at My table in My kingdom, and sit on thrones judging the twelve tribes of Israel." (Lk 22:28-30)[7]

The apocalypse of Saint John recorded in the book of Revelation confirms this teaching of the Lord. The "marriage supper of the Lamb" is announced to come at the end of the ages, and all who are invited to share in God's hospitality are called blessed.

"Hallelujah! For the Lord our God the Almighty reigns. Let us rejoice and exult and give Him the glory, for the marriage of the Lamb has come, and His Bride has made herself ready; it was granted her to be clothed with fine linen, bright and pure"—for the fine linen

[6]See, for example, Mt 22:1-13; 25:1-13; Lk 14:1-24; 15:11-32.
[7]See also Mt 8:11-12.

is the righteous deeds of the saints. And the angel said to me, "Write this, Blessed are those who are invited to the marriage supper of the Lamb." And he said to me, "These are true words of God." (Rev 19:6-9)

22

What Shall We Offer You, O Christ?

The Church's liturgy of the winter festal season speaks not only of the hospitality which the Son of God comes to give to His people. It tells also of the hospitality which He hopes to receive from them when He comes. The songs and hymns of the services call the faithful to welcome God's Son, to accept Him, to greet Him, to go forth to meet Him.

> The most wise Lord comes to be born,
> Receiving hospitality from His own creatures.
> Let us also receive Him,
> That this divine Child in the cave may make us His guests
> In the paradise of delights![1]

Not only are human beings who are made in God's image and likeness called to prepare the Lord's coming and to welcome Him into the world which He made, but all of God's creatures are invited to join in the reception of their Master. The liturgy proclaims that the whole of creation necessarily participates in the incarnation of its Lord, and that without this active and voluntary participation, the Master literally could not come.

The incarnation of God's Son is a cooperative effort. It is a collaboration between the Creator and His creatures. It is a *synergy* between God the Father, Son, and Holy Spirit on the one side, and all of the angels and animals and elements on the other, with human persons at the center as the main mediators between heaven and earth, being those for whom

[1]Matins of the first day of the prefeast of the Nativity, December 20.

the world was made and to whom it is given. There can be
no coming of the Son of God, no incarnation of the Divine
Word, no birth of Jesus unless everyone and everything cheer-
fully and gratefully join into the act. This is not only true
"physically" in history, but it is also true "mystically" in our
spiritual lives.

One of the beloved songs of the Orthodox Nativity season
is sung at vespers on Christmas eve. Those who are familiar
with the liturgy, especially the children who are just becoming
aware of its beauty and power, often wait for this hymn
and rejoice when they sing it for it tells in the most touching
way of the all-embracing participation of creatures in the
Creator's coming.

> What shall we offer You, O Christ,
> Who for our sake has appeared on the earth as a man?
> Every creature which You have made offers You thanks.
> The angels offer You a song.
> The heavens, their star.
> The wise men, their gifts.
> The shepherds, their wonder.
> The earth, its cave.
> The wilderness, the manger.
> And we offer You a Virgin Mother.
> O Pre-eternal God, have mercy on us![2]

How wonderful it is to contemplate the celestial and
cosmic cooperation involved in the coming of the Lord. And
how significant it is to see what we humans have to offer. We
provide the earthly mother without whom God's Son could
not be born as a man. This is the Church's dogma.

The Orthodox Church teaches that it is unreasonable,
impious, and even blasphemous to think that God could
choose just any woman to be the mother of His Son or that the
Lord could be born without, or even against, the free and
voluntary cooperation of the one who bore Him. Or, even
worse, that He could simply "choose a womb" from which to
be born "as water passing through a pipe," as some early

---

[2]Vespers of the eve of the feast of the Nativity, December 25.

Christian heretics claimed in their misguided zeal to defend the sovereignty and power of God "who does whatever He wills." It is rather considered to be the greatest glory of creatures that they all give thanks to God in a manner appropriate to their being by providing the conditions for His becoming one of them Himself. Little did the three young men in the fiery furnace of Babylon realize to what glory creatures were to come in the Messianic age when they called all to bless the Lord and to praise and exalt Him forever.[3] And little did any child of Adam and Eve realize to what glory human beings would come when one of their own, called the "new Eve," would become truly "Theotokos" by giving birth to a man who is the divine Son of God.[4]

The songs of Christ's birth, and perhaps even more so, as we shall see, those of His baptism in the Jordan, repeat the theme again and again in many different ways. All creation participates in the Lord's appearance on earth. And all creation participates in the saving sanctification which He brings.

> With the shepherds and angels
> They prepare the way of the Lord.
> The star shines brightly;
> The cavern is radiant.
> The wise men come with gifts;
>
> Come, O Bethlehem,
> Anoint the holy manger,
> For the Master comes to you,
> Sanctifying your wood with His own divinity.[5]

The families of the nations

[3]Dan 3:57-90, LXX; "The Song of the Three Young Men," verses 35-68, Common Bible. For the Orthodox, this song is part of the canonical scriptures of the Old Testament, and so, part of the Bible. In Western editions of the Scriptures it is printed in the Old Testament Apocrypha.

[4]See above, pp 95-96. Very early in Christian tradition, e.g., in the writings of Saint Irenaeas of Lyons who died about 200 AD, Mary is called the "new Eve" because she heard the good angel and obeyed God who sent Him, thus becoming the "birthgiver of God" (in Greek, *Theotokos*), who is truly the "mother of all living" (see Gen 3:20).

[5]Matins of the second day of the prefeast of the Nativity, December 21.

Offer glory and praise.
The wise men come with gifts;
The shepherds watch in the fields,
Joyfully preparing the way.

Your hills and mountains,
You plains and valleys,
You rivers and all creation,
Magnify your Lord
Who comes for your sake to be born.[6]

Give good works to the manger of our souls, O Lord,
That with faces bright and shining
We may sing to You who comes to be born:
"Bless the Lord, O works of the Lord!"[7]

---

[6]Vespers of the third day of the prefeast of the Nativity, December 22.
[7]Compline of the second day of the prefeast of the Nativity, December 21.

23

Glad Tidings of Great Joy

The birth of Jesus is announced to the world as a proclamation of great joy. The archangel Gabriel comes first to Zacharias the priest when he is offering incense at the altar and tells him that his wife Elizabeth will give birth to a son who will be the forerunner of the Messiah. "You will have joy and gladness," he tells him, "and many will rejoice at his birth" (Lk 1:14). The same messenger of the Lord comes to the Virgin Mary, and the message is the same. Mary's "soul magnifies the Lord," and her "spirit rejoices in God" her Savior (Lk 1:46-47). For her Child will be the Messiah Himself, "called the Son of the Most High," to whom the Lord God will give "the throne of His father David, and He shall reign over the house of Jacob forever; and of His kingdom there will be no end" (Lk 1:32-33). And the birth is announced to the world again by the angel of the Lord. It is an announcement of "glad tidings of great joy which shall be to all people (Lk 2:10).

And she gave birth to her first-born Son and wrapped Him in swaddling cloths, and laid Him in a manger, because there was no place for them in the inn. And in that region there were shepherds out in the field, keeping watch over their flock by night. And an angel of the Lord appeared to them, and the glory of the Lord shone around them, and they were filled with fear. And the angel said to them, "Be not afraid; for behold, I bring you good news of a great joy which will come to all the people; for to you is born this day in the city of David a Savior, who is Christ the Lord. And

this will be a sign for you: you will find a babe
wrapped in swaddling cloths and lying in a manger."
And suddenly there was with the angel a multitude of
the heavenly host praising God and saying, "Glory to
God in the highest, and on earth peace, good will
among men!" (Lk 2:7-14)

The joy of the Messiah's appearance abounds in the
Church's liturgical services of the Winter Pascha. When the
"Hail" of the angelic salutation is translated "Rejoice," as it
often is in the Church services since in Greek that is what it
literally means, there is an even greater presence of the "good
news of great joy" for the faithful, since they, together with
the whole of creation, are greeted with this salutation again
and again in the songs of the festal celebration.

> Let creation exceedingly rejoice,
> For the Creator fashions Himself as a creature.
> And he who was before all things now manifests Himself
>   as God newly revealed.
> Let the wise men go to meet Him with their gifts;
> Let the shepherds clap their hands in faith at the wonder;
> and let mortal men join the angels with rejoicing.[1]

> Be joyful, O earth!
> Behold, Christ draws near to be born in Bethlehem.
> Be glad, O sea!
> And dance for joy, O company of prophets,
> For today you behold the fulfillment of your words.
> Rejoice, all you righteous!

> Let the kings of the whole earth sing with rejoicing,
> And let the nations be in exceeding joy!
> Mountains, hills, and valleys,
> Rivers, seas, and the whole of creation:
> Magnify the Lord who now is born.

> Rejoice, O Virgin,

[1]Compline of the final day of the prefeast of the Nativity, December 24.

The Theotokos who of the Holy Spirit
Has borne Life into the world
For the salvation of all![2]

One of the most devastating accusations that can be made against Christians is that they have no joy. Joyless Christians are a contradiction in terms. People who are bitter, complaining, condemning, accusing, dissatisfied, and depressed are certainly not Christians. They can only be people whose life is untouched by grace, people whose existence is confined to the suffocating limitations of "this world" whose "ruler" is the devil and whose "form . . . is passing away" (Jn 12:31; 1 Cor 7:31). They cannot possibly be those who belong to Christ and the kingdom of God. For Christians by definition have Christ's "joy fulfilled in themselves" (Jn 17:13). They are people whose joy, which no one can take away, is literally full and complete (Jn 15:11; 16:22, 24).

In his famous book *For the Life of the World,* Father Alexander Schmemann speaks about the joy of Christians. From its very beginning, he says,

Christianity has been the proclamation of joy, of the only possible joy on earth. It rendered impossible all joy we usually think of as possible. But within this impossibility, at the very bottom of this darkness, it announced and conveyed a new all-embracing joy, and with this joy it transformed the End into a Beginning. Without the proclamation of this joy Christianity is incomprehensible. It is only as joy that the Church was victorious in the world, and it lost the world when it lost that joy, and ceased to be a credible witness to it. Of all accusations against Christians, the most terrible one was uttered by Nietzsche when he said that Christians had no joy.[3]

Farther Alexander goes on to say that before Christians can do anything else with all of their "programs and missions,

[2]Matins of the final day of the prefeast of the Nativity, December 24.
[3]*For the Life of the World,* p. 24.

projects and techniques," they "must recover the meaning of this great joy." He says that joy "is not something one can define or analyze. One enters into joy. 'Enter thou into the joy of thy lord' (Mt. 25:21)," And one enters into this joy, this exceeding great joy, he insists, only by entering into the liturgical, eucharistic life of the Church herself. Here, and only here, as in the celebration of the Nativity of Christ and His Epiphany in the world, can a person partake of that joyful reality for which the world itself was created in the beginning.

> Come, let us greatly rejoice in the Lord,
> As we tell of this present mystery!
> The dividing wall has been destroyed;
> The flaming sword turns back;
> The cherubim withdraw from the Tree of Life;
> And I partake of the delight of paradise,
> From which I was cast away through disobedience.
> For the Express Image of the Father,
> The very Imprint of His Eternity,
> Takes the form of a slave,
> And without undergoing change [to His divinity],
> He comes forth from a mother who has not known a man.
> For what He was, He remains: True God.
> And what He was not, He takes upon Himself,
> Becoming man out of His love for man.
> To Him let us cry aloud:
> O God born of a Virgin, have mercy on us![4]

> All the angels in heaven rejoice
> And greatly celebrate today.
> The whole creation leaps for joy,
> For the Savior and Lord is born in Bethlehem
> Every error of idolatry has ceased,
> And Christ reigns throughout all ages.[5]

[4]The first verse sung on "Lord, I Call" at the vesperal liturgy on the eve of the feast of the Nativity.

[5]Litya verse at compline of the feast of the Nativity. Because the vespers of the feast is a eucharistic liturgy with the anaphora of Saint Basil the Great, the festal vigil of the Nativity begins with compline.

24

Peace on Earth, Good Will Toward Men

When the angel of the Lord brought the "glad tidings of great joy" of Christ's birth to the shepherds in the fields, there appeared also "a multitude of the heavenly host praising God, and saying, Glory to God in the highest, and on earth peace, good will toward men" (Lk 2:13-14, KJV). The songs of the Orthodox church services, like those of the Christian West, put this doxology of the angelic choir in the mouths of the faithful again and again.

Glory to God in the highest, and on earth peace!
Today Bethlehem receives Him who reigns forever
    with the Father.
Today angels glorify the newborn babe in hymns worthy
    of God:
Glory to God in the highest!
And on earth peace, good will toward men![1]

The original Greek version of this biblical text, which the Church has received and which she uses in her liturgy, reads "peace on earth, good will towards men," and not "peace on earth to men of good will." The theological point here is an important one. The teaching is not that God gives His peace to people who have good will. It is rather that God

[1]Matins of the feast of the Nativity. The verse, *Glory to God in the highest, and on earth peace, good will toward men,* is used as the first line of the great and small doxologies, chanted daily at Orthodox matins and compline. It also is used daily at matins before the recitation of the six morning psalms. And it is said quietly by the priest at the beginning of the eucharistic liturgy.

gives His peace and His good will to all people through His
Son, the Messiah-Christ.[2]

The coming of Jesus inaugerates the final and everlasting
"covenant of peace" foretold by the prophets of Israel.

> For the mountains may depart
>   and the hills be removed,
> but My steadfast love shall not depart from you,
>   and My covenant of peace shall not be removed . . .
>   (Is 54:10)

> Incline your ear and come to Me;
>   hear, that your soul may live;
> and I will make with you an everlasting covenant,
>   My steadfast, sure love for David. (Is 55:3)

> I will make with them an everlasting covenant,
>   that I will not turn away from doing good to them;
> and I will put the fear of Me in their hearts,
>   that they may not turn from Me.
> I will rejoice in doing them good,
>   and I will plant them in this land in faithfulness,
>   with all My heart and all My soul. (Jer 32:40-41)

> My servant David shall be king over them; and they
> shall all have one shepherd. They shall follow My
> ordinances and be careful to observe My statutes. They
> shall dwell in the land where your fathers dwelt that
> I gave to My servant Jacob; they and their children
> and their children's children shall dwell there for
> ever; and David My servant shall be their prince for
> ever. I will make a covenant of peace with them; it
> shall be an everlasting covenant with them; and I will
> bless them and multiply them, and will set My sanc-

---

[2]In the original Greek, the word "towards" is literally "in" or "among."
The word "good will," sometimes translated in the service as "good pleasure,"
is one word in Greek: *eudokia*. It is often used in Orthodox theology as a
synonym for God's free and voluntary action. Thus, for example, God is said
to have a Son and a Holy Spirit by *nature* (*ousia*), but He creates the world
and saves it by His *good will* (*evdokia*).

tuary in the midst of them for evermore. My dwelling place shall be with them; and I will be their God, and they shall be My people. Then the nations will know that I the Lord sanctify Israel, when My sanctuary is in the midst of them for evermore. (Ezek 37:24-28)

The peace of God which Jesus brings to the world is not worldly peace. It is, as the Orthodox liturgy prays in the great litany, the "peace from above."[3] The Lord referred specifically to this peace, the *shalom* of God, when He told His disciples before His passion: "Peace I leave with you; My peace I give to you; not as the world gives do I give to you" (Jn 14:27). How sad it is that many people still do not understand this, including many Christians and many Christian preachers who may be charged with misguidance and malpractice when they announce each year at Christmastime that Jesus brought peace to the world almost two thousand years ago, and still there is hostility and war among the people of the earth!

As a matter of plain fact, Jesus Christ never promised to bring peace to the earth in the sense that nations would no longer fight with one another and that individuals would no longer quarrel. Such a peace is promised only at the end of the ages when the Messiah who was crucified comes in glory to establish the kingdom of God His Father. Then, and only then, will the great and everlasting *shalom* of the Lord foretold by the prophets be established.[4] Until then, strife and struggle remain. And Jesus Himself, as He foretold, will remain a great reason for much of it.

Do not think that I have come to bring peace on earth; I have not come to bring peace, but a sword. For I

[3]*Peace* is a crucial word in Christian liturgy. The "Peace be unto all" directed to the faithful at each critical moment in the services is the condition for their participation in the action of God. All liturgical worship of the Church begins with an invocation of this peace: "In peace, let us pray to the Lord . . . For the peace from above and for the salvation of our souls, let us pray to the Lord. . . . For the peace of the whole world, for the welfare of God's holy churches, and for the union of all, let us pray to the Lord. . . ."

[4]See Is 9:6-7; 54-57; Mic 4-5; Ezek 34-37.

have come to set a man against his father, and a
daughter against her mother, and a daughter-in-law
against her mother-in-law; and a man's foes will be
those of his own household. He who loves father or
mother more than Me is not worthy of Me; and he
who loves son or daughter more than Me is not worthy
of Me; and he who does not take his cross and follow
Me is not worthy of Me. He who finds his life will
lose it, and he who loses his life for My sake will find
it. (Mt 10:34-39)

Christian saints through the ages bear witness that the
peace of God has entered the world in Jesus because they
receive this peace and live by it as the content of their lives.
In a real sense, all that Christians have to offer the world is
God's peace which, with His righteousness and joy in the
Holy Spirit, constitutes the kingdom of God (see Rom 14:17).
"Acquire the spirit of peace," says Saint Seraphim of Sarov,
"and you will save thousands around you." Without this
divine peace, whatever one's message and deeds, nothing
divine and eternal will result and remain.

But Christian saints also cause hostility and strife. They
are sources of scandal and causes of contention. They witness
to the truth of Jesus' words that as He was hated and persecuted, so also His faithful followers will be arrested, imprisoned, tortured, and killed—not only by those who openly
hate both Him and His Father, but by those who have come
to the point where they commit murder and think that they
are "offering service to God" (Jn 16:2).

If the world hates you, know that it has hated Me
before it hated you. If you were of the world, the
world would love its own; but because you are not of
the world, but I chose you out of the world, therefore
the world hates you. Remember the word that I said
to you, "A servant is not greater than his master." If
they persecuted Me, they will persecute you; if they
kept My word, they will keep yours also. But all this

they will do to you on My account, because they do not
know Him who sent Me. (Jn 15:18-21)

Things are not different today than they ever were. Ex-
ternal conditions may change, but the inner spiritual conditions remain the same. Jesus brought God's peace and good
will to the world. He brought God's kingdom. But until it is
established in power at the end of the ages, the struggle goes
on.

Today heaven and earth are united, for Christ is born.
Today God has come to earth, and man ascends to heaven.
Today God, who by nature cannot be seen,
Is seen in the flesh for our sake.
Let us glorify Him, crying:
Glory to God in the highest, and on earth peace!
Your coming has brought peace to us:
Glory to You, our Savior[5]

"Glory to God in the highest,"
I hear the angels sing today in Bethlehem.
Glory to Him whose good pleasure it was
That peace should come on earth!
The Virgin is now more spacious than the heavens.
Light has shone on those in darkness;
It has exalted the lowly, who sing like the angels:
Glory to God in the highest!

---

[5]Litya verses at compline of the feast of the Nativity.

25

God Is With Us!

The vigil services of Christmas and Epiphany begin with the chanting of great compline, at the heart of which is the solemn singing of the canticle from the prophet Isaiah.

God is with us!
Understand all nations,
And submit yourselves,
For God is with us!

Hear this, even to the farthest bounds of the earth.
Submit yourselves, O mighty ones;
If you rise up again in your might,
You will be again overthrown.
The Lord shall destroy all who take counsel together,
And the word which you speak shall not abide with you.
For we do not fear your terror,
And we are not troubled.
But we will ascribe holiness to the Lord our God
And Him we will fear.
And if I put my trust in Him
He shall be my sanctification.
I will set my hope on Him
And through Him I shall be saved,
Lo, I and the children whom God has given me.
The people who walked in darkness have seen a great
    light.
Those who dwelt in a land of deep darkness, on them
    has light shined.
For to us a Child is born,

To us a Son is given.
And the government shall be upon His shoulder,
And of His peace there will be no end.
And His name shall be called the Angel of the
    Great Council;
Wonderful; Counsellor;
The Mighty God, the Everlasting Father;
The Prince of Peace;
The Father of the world to come!
(Is 8:9-10, 17-18; 9:2, 6-7 LXX)[1]

These lines of the prophetic writing, which are included in many of the songs of the services of the Winter Pascha, are also referred to directly in the Gospel according to Saint Matthew.

Now the birth of Jesus Christ took place in this way. When His mother Mary had been betrothed to Joseph, before they came together she was found to be with child of the Holy Spirit; and her husband Joseph, being a just man and unwilling to put her to shame, resolved to divorce her quietly. But as he considered this, behold, an angel of the Lord appeared to him in a dream, saying, "Joseph, son of David, do not fear to take Mary your wife, for that which is conceived in her is of the Holy Spirit; she will bear a son, and you shall call His name Jesus, for He will save His people from their sins." All this took place to fulfil what the Lord had spoken by the prophet: "Behold, a virgin shall conceive and bear a son, and His name shall be called Emmanuel" (which means, God with us). (Mt 1:18-23; IS 7:14)

It once happened that a person hearing the Orthodox vigil on Christmas for the first time in English was greatly

---

[1]This translation is from the Church's service book, following the Septuagint text. Some people think that the Isaiah canticle is specifically prescribed for the festivals of the Lord's Nativity and Epiphany, but actually the song is part of great compline whenever it is chanted, as, for example, on the evenings of the first week of Great Lent.

angered by the singing of this prophetic canticle. She came
to the priest, very upset, and asked him how such a terrible
song could be sung in church. When the priest asked her
which song she meant, and discovered which it was, he was
surprised that this woman, who was a member of the Orthodox
Church, had never heard the song before. It turned out that
she had indeed heard it, but had never understood its meaning
clearly because of the foreign language in which the services
had been celebrated. Her difficulty was with the fact that the
verse said, "God is with us!" and that it called all people to
understand and submit themselves. How unbelievably pre-
sumptuous, she declared, that the Orthodox would solemnly
proclaim that God was with them and then be even more
arrogant in demanding the others understand and submit!
Although the woman was gravely mistaken in her interpretation of the song, her attitude betrayed a common approach
to religion in North America, where no church is supposed
to think itself truer than others, and where submission in any
form is considered to be degrading and demeaning.

The point of Isaiah's canticle is not that God is with one
particular group of people and not another. The point is rather
that God is with all people in the coming of the promised
Messiah. The writings of the prophet himself make this
teaching quite clear, as the interpretation of the gospels and
the apostolic writings of the Christian New Testament plainly
testify.

> Behold My servant, whom I uphold, My chosen, in
> whom My soul delights; I have put My Spirit upon
> him, he will bring forth justice to the nations. He
> will not cry or lift up his voice, or make it heard in the
> street; a bruised reed he will not break, and a dimly
> burning wick he will not quench; he will faithfully
> bring forth justice. He will not fail or be discouraged
> till he has established justice in the earth; and the
> coastlands wait for his law. Thus says God, the Lord,
> who created the heavens and stretched them out, who
> spread forth the earth and what comes from it, who
> gives breath to the people upon it and spirit to those

who walk in it: "I am the Lord, I have called you in
righteousness, I have taken you by the hand and kept
you; I have given you as a covenant to the people, a
light to the nations, to open the eyes that are blind,
to bring out the prisoners from the dungeon, from the
prison those who sit in darkness. I am the Lord, that is
My name; My glory I give to no other, nor My praise
to graven images. Behold, the former things have come
to pass, and new things I now declare; before they
spring forth I tell you of them." (Is 42:1-9)

Jesus is the chosen servant of God. He is the one anointed
with God's Spirit. The very word "Messiah" means the
Anointed One. He is the light to the nations. In Him shall all
of the gentiles hope.[2] For, as the Lord says through Isaiah, in
a line quoted by Saint Paul, "I was ready to be sought by those
who did not ask for Me; I was ready to be found by those
who did not seek Me. I said, 'Here am I, here am I,' to a
nation that did not call on My name" (Is 65:1; Rom 10:20-
21).

When the Christ appears on earth, God is truly with us,
all of us; not only with the Jews but with the gentiles, not
only with the Orthodox Christians and Christians generally
but with all people, including those who do not ask for Him
and do not seek Him. All peoples and nations are called to
understand this and to submit to it, not for God's sake but
for their own. It is their honor, not their humiliation. It is
their dignity, not their degradation. It is their freedom, not
their enslavement. It is their very life.

All things have been delivered to Me by My Father;
and no one knows the Son except the Father, and no
one knows the Father except the Son and any one to
whom the Son chooses to reveal Him. Come to Me, all
who labor and are heavy laden, and I will give you
rest. Take My yoke upon you, and learn from Me;
for I am gentle and lowly in heart, and you will find

[2]See Mt 4:15-16, 12:18-21; Lk 2:29-32, 3:4-6; 4:18-19.

rest for your souls. For My yoke is easy, and My burden is light. (Mt 11:27-30)

This is the message of the Winter Pascha. God is with us on earth. He is in our very midst as the man Jesus, whose name is Emmanuel. He has revealed His unknowable, inconceivable, ineffable, invisible nature in the most tangible way: as the Child who is born for us, as the Son who is given to us. To understand this and to submit to it is man's greatest glory and joy.

Today the Virgin gives birth to the Transcendent One,
And the earth offers a cave to the Unapproachable One.
Angels with shepherds glorify Him;
The wise men journey with a star;
Since for our sake the Eternal God was born as a little
    Child![3]

---

[3]Kontakion of the feast of the Nativity.

26

The Sun of Righteousness

One of the titles of the Messiah in the prophetic writings of the Bible is the Sun of Righteousness. It is found in the prophet Malachi.

> For behold, the day comes, burning like an oven, when all the arrogant and all evildoers will be stubble; the day that comes shall burn them up, says the Lord of hosts, so that it will leave them neither root nor branch. But for you who fear My name, the Sun of Righteousness shall rise, with healing in its wings. You shall go forth leaping like calves from the stall. And you shall tread down the wicked, for they will be ashes under the soles of your feet, on the day when I act, says the Lord of hosts. (Mal 4:1-3)

God Himself is called the Sun in the biblical writings (see Ps 84:11). As the source of light, and Light itself, God gives this same title to His only-begotten Son who appears on earth as the dawn of a new day, the Day of the Lord which enlightens those who sit in darkness and in the land of the shadow of death (see Is 9:2, 42:6-7). An eloquent witness to this teaching is found in Saint Luke's gospel, in the song of Zacharias, the father of John the Baptist.

> And you, child, will be called the prophet of the
>   Most High;
> For you will go before the Lord to prepare His ways,
> To give knowledge of salvation to His people
> In the forgiveness of their sins,

Through the tender mercy of our God,
When the day shall dawn upon us from on high
To give light to those who sit in darkness and in the
    shadow of death,
To guide our feet into the way of peace. (Lk 1:76-79)

This translation of the text is a bit free in its rendering.
Literally it says that the "Orient from on high" shall visit us
in the world, referring to Jesus Christ. This expression is used
in the main hymn of the feast of the Nativity in the Orthodox
Church, and for a very specific historical reason.[1]

Originally there was but one festival in the Christian
Church for the Lord's appearing. It was called the "festival
of lights" and it was connected both to the Jewish festival
of the season, as well as to the pagan celebration which took
place at the time of year when the sun stopped its southern
march and began to move again towards the north, symbolizing the victory of light over darkness in the natural order.
This feast for the Christians was the feast of *Epiphany*,
which literally means "appearing" or "manifestation," also
called *Theophany*, which literally means the appearance or
the manifestation of God, and was kept on January 6.[2] It
was given this name, obviously, because God appeared on
earth in the person of His Son, and manifested His glory
in Him who called Himself the "light of the world."

Again Jesus spoke to them, saying, "I am the light of
the world; he who follows Me will not walk in darkness, but will have the light of life." (Jn 8:12)

"As long as I am in the world, I am the light of the
world." (Jn 9:5)

[1]The word "orient" is *anatolia* in Greek, which literally means "east."
The King James version of the Bible translates it as "dayspring."

[2]The Armenian Church to this day celebrates but one festival of the Lord's
Coming, on January 6. This should not be confused with the celebration of
Christ's Nativity on January 7 by some Orthodox Churches, for example
those in the USSR, which is December 25 according to the Julian calendar
which these churches still use.

"I have come as light into the world, that whoever believes in Me may not remain in darkness." (Jn 12:46)

These words from Saint John's gospel hark back to the prologue of the same book where Jesus is identified with God's divine Word, an identification made many times in the liturgical services of the Winter Pascha.

In the beginning was the Word, and the Word was with God, and the Word was God. He was in the beginning with God; all things were made through Him, and without Him was not anything made that was made. In Him was life, and the life was the light of men. The light shines in the darkness, and the darkness has not overcome it. There was a man sent from God, whose name was John. He came for testimony, to bear witness to the light, that all might believe through him. He was not the light, but came to bear witness to the light. The true light that enlightens every man was coming into the world. . . . And the Word became flesh and dwelt among us, full of grace and truth; we have beheld His glory, glory as of the only Son from the Father. (Jn 1:1-14)

The separate celebration of Jesus' nativity apart from the one general celebration of His appearance on earth—which originally included all aspects of His coming, from His birth to His public manifestation at His baptism in the river Jordan—was consciously done by the Christian Church, first in the West and later in the East, to offset the pagan holiday of the "Nativity of the Invincible Sun." This pagan festival was celebrated on the twenty-fifth of December. It was a day of religious observance for those who worshipped the heavenly bodies, particularly the sun, as gods. When pagans were liberated from this worship and were blessed to adore the true God as Christians, it was only natural that the Church would replace the erroneous festival with the true one, thus giving genuine significance to a day which was already special

in the life of many of its new members. It appears that the
main hymn of the feast of Christ's Nativity in the Eastern
Church was formulated as a conscious polemic against paganism, with a very pointed flaunting of the fact that those who
formerly worshipped the stars, including the sun, were taught
by a star to worship the True Sun, God's Son Jesus, who
gives, and *is*, the True Light.

> Your Nativity, O Christ our God,
> Has shown to the world the light of wisdom
> For by it those who worshipped the stars
> Were taught by a star to adore You,
> The Sun of Righteousness,
> And to know You, the Orient from on high.
> O Lord, glory to You![3]

Some people fault the Christian Church for establishing
the feast of Christ's birth on the day of the "birth of the
sun." Certain Christian sects even oppose the celebration.
Orthodox Christians believe that it was an act inspired by
the Holy Spirit. God has sent His Son into the world for its
sanctification and salvation. The Messiah has come "not to
condemn the world," with its feeble and misguided attempts
to find life's meaning, "but that the world might be saved
through Him" (Jn 3:17). For, as the apostle Paul has written,
"it is the God who said 'Let light shine out of darkness,' who
has shone in our hearts to give the light of the knowledge of
the glory of God in the face [literally, *person*] of Christ" (2
Cor 4:6).

> The Magi who had been led on their way by a divine star
> Stood before You in wonder at Your marvelous birth;
> And bearing gifts, they see the Sun
> Who rose from the virgin cloud.

---

[3]Troparion of the feast of the Nativity. The name "Orient" for the Messiah
is also proclaimed in a popular Orthodox church hymn which is sung at
many services, but is most widely identified with weddings and ordinations:
Rejoice, O Isaiah, a virgin is with child, and shall bear a son, Emmanuel, both
God and man. And Orient is His Name, whom magnifying, we call the
Virgin blessed.

Let the people who sat in darkness
See shining forth the Light that knows no evening,
Him whom the star once manifested
To the fire-worshipping Persian kings.[4]

You have shone forth a Virgin,
O Spiritual Sun of Righteousness,
And a star revealed You,
Whom nothing can contain,
Contained with a cave.
You have led the Magi to worship You,
And joining with them we magnify You.
O Giver of Life, glory to You.[5]

Our Savior, the Dayspring from the East,
Has visited us from on high;
And we who were in darkness and shadow
Have found the Truth.
For the Lord is born of a Virgin![6]

[4]Matins of the final day of the prefeast of the Nativity, December 24. See Rev 21:23-25: "And the city has no need of sun or moon to shine upon it, for the glory of God is its light, and its lamp is the Lamb [i.e., Christ]. By its light shall the nations walk; and the kings of the earth shall bring their glory into it, and its gates shall never be shut by day—and there shall be no night there . . ."

[5]Vespers of the feast of the Nativity.

[6]The hymn of light at matins of the feast of the Nativity. See above, note 1.

27

The Ever-Virgin Mary

The gospels teach and the liturgy proclaims that Jesus Christ was born on earth from the Virgin Mary. According to the "mind of Christ" which is given to believers by the indwelling of God's Holy Spirit (see 1 Cor 2), it is evident that it could not be otherwise. The reason is simple. Jesus is the Son of God. God is His Father from all eternity. If there is anything unique, original, totally unprecedented in the scriptures, and absolutely undeniable about the teaching of Jesus Himself, it is this: He, and only He, can call the Most High God, *Abba, Father!* He does so in the pages of the gospels nearly two hundred times.

Jesus' father is God. Therefore He can have no human father. He has to be born of a virgin. Saint Matthew sees the virgin birth as the fulfillment of the words of the prophet Isaiah: "Behold, a virgin shall conceive and bear a son, and his name shall be called Emmanuel (which means, God with us)" (Mt 1:23; Is 7:14). Although scholars dispute the word "virgin" in this text, saying that it can also mean "young woman," it is clear from the Greek word used by the evangelist, as well as from his entire narrative, that he literally means a virgin who has had no intercourse with a human husband.[1]

---

[1]Some also claim that the Isaiah text has nothing to do with the birth of Jesus but indicates a happening in the prophet's own time. Whether or not this is so has little to do with the use of the text in the gospels since, in classical Christian interpretation, the prophets need not know the ultimate meaning of their words, and many historical events in Israel's history are taken as "types" or "figures" of events to take place later, with a totally new meaning, in the messianic age. It is interesting to note that the prophet's words to Ahaz, "The Lord Himself will give you a sign," have given rise in Orthodox tradition to the name for the icon of the Virgin Mary with her

Although there are certain discrepancies between the infancy narratives in the gospels of Saint Matthew and Saint Luke, there is no discrepancy at all concerning the virgin birth of Jesus. Saint Luke gives the story in greatest detail. Mary asks the angel directly about how the birth can take place when she says, "I have no husband" (Lk 1:34). We all know the angel's answer.

"The Holy Spirit will come upon you,
and the power of the Most High will overshadow you;
therefore the child to be born will be called holy,
    the Son of God." (Lk 1:35)

Church tradition claims that Saint Luke received the story of Christ's birth from Mary herself, seeing in his statement, "and His mother kept all these things in her heart," a not-so-veiled reference to the source of his information (Lk 2:51). But whatever the case, his teaching is clear. The Messiah is God's Son who has no human father (see Lk 3:23).

A great and marvelous wonder has happened today:
A virgin bears a child
And her womb suffers no corruption.
The Word is made flesh
Yet does not cease to dwell with the Father.
Angels with shepherds give glory,
And with them we cry aloud:
Glory to God in the highest, and on earth peace.[2]

hands extended in the praying position and the Christ Child depicted within her. It is called the "Theotokos of the Sign," or simply the icon of "the Sign."

[2]Compline of the feast of the Nativity. The use of expressions such as "without corruption" or "without defilement" for the birth of Christ and the womb of Mary are "ontological" not "ethical" statements. The point is that Christ's birth takes place in a miraculous manner, leaving Mary's virginity intact. This in no way compromises the reality of the birth as "opening Mary's womb" since the gospel claims that her womb was opened (Lk 2:23), and the icons of the feast depict midwives washing the newborn Christ Child. The Church opposes any attempt to deny, or even to minimize, the genuiness of Christ's humanity, which is officially defined by the fourth ecumenical council in Chalcedon as identical to our own. See above, pp. 95-96.

Why are you filled with wonder, O Mary?
Why are you amazed at what has happened in you?
"I have given birth in time to the timeless Son,
Yet I do not understand how I conceived Him.
I have not known a man;
How then could I bear a child?
Who has ever seen a birth without seed?
But as it is written:
When God wills, the order of nature is overcome."
Christ is born of the Virgin in Bethlehem of Judea![3]

It is also the Church's teaching, following the scripture, that Mary remained a virgin all of her life. She never knew a man. And she never had any other children besides the Lord Jesus. Once again, this conviction is not only defended on the basis of the biblical record, but it is also understood to be a theological truth inspired by the Holy Spirit which is mystically proper and spiritually evident to those with "the mind of Christ" (1 Cor 2:16).[4]

The Bible never mentions Mary having any children but Jesus. There is no text that even remotely indicates such a thing. Jesus' "brothers and sisters" are mentioned, but there is no explicit statement that these are Mary's children. The traditional interpretation from the earliest times in the Church is that these are either cousins of Jesus or children of Joseph by another marriage.[5] It is known that Joseph was much older than Mary, and that he died before Jesus began to preach. When hanging on the Cross, Jesus formally commended His mother to the beloved disciple John, which would have been a meaningless act if his "brethren" were in fact Mary's own children (Jn 19:26-27).

The spiritual evidence and mystical meaning of Mary's

[3]Matins of the feast of the Nativity.

[4]The text in Saint Matthew's gospel that Joseph "knew her not until she had borne a son" (Mt 1:25) is considered to be a semitic idiom which in no way implies that he "knew her" after the son was born. Saint John Chrysostom, himself from Antioch, presents other such idioms from the Bible which illustrate this point. See Chrysostom, *On Matthew*, homily V, 5-6.

[5]The Church solemnly affirms that Jesus had "brothers and sisters," calling Saint James, who is liturgically celebrated on the Sunday after the Nativity, "the brother of the Lord."

ever-virginity, which was witnessed as Church dogma by the fifth ecumenical council in 553 and is endlessly repeated in the Church's liturgical worship, is overpowering to the minds and hearts of believers. It is simply inconceivable to the saints that the woman who gave birth by the Holy Spirit to God's divine Son, His Word and Wisdom, His Express Image and the Radiance of His Glory, should then proceed normally to mother more children in the usual manner. There is no depreciation of childbirth here, and certainly no disgust for the sexual union.[6] There is rather the clear understanding of the uniqueness of Mary, the one "blessed among women," whom "all generations will call . . . blessed," given to the Church as the living image of all those who are saved because they "hear the word of God and keep it" (Lk 1:42, 48; 11:28). The place of Mary in God's plan of salvation affirms her ever-virginity more than any particular biblical text or any specific scriptural reference for those who have come to know her in the mystical life of the Church.

> Behold, the Virgin, as was said of old,
> Has conceived in her womb
> And has brought forth God as a man,
> Yet she remains still a virgin.
> Being reconciled to God through her,
> Let us sinners sing her praises,
> For truly she is Theotokos.[7]

> How is He contained in a womb
> Whom nothing can contain?
> How can He be held in the arms of His mother
> Who remains forever in the bosom of His Father?
> It is according to His good will,
> As He knows and as He desires!
> For being without flesh,
> He of His own good will has been made flesh;
> And HE WHO IS has for our sake become what
>   He was not.

[6]See above, pp. 41-43.
[7]Matins of the feast of the Nativity.

He has shared our nature without departing from His own.
Desiring to fill the world on high with citizens,
Christ has undergone a twofold birth![8]

He who before the morning star
Was begotten of the Father without a mother,
Is made flesh on earth today without a father from you.
A star announces the glad tidings to the wise men,
While angels with shepherds sing the praises of your
     child-bearing without corruption,
You who are full of grace![9]

[8]Matins of the feast of the Nativity and sung again at matins on the third day of Christmas, the feast of Saint Stephen, the first martyr. The HE WHO IS in the hymn is a reference to God's Name which was revealed to Moses (see Ex 3:14).

[9]Kontakion of the second day of the Nativity, the feast of the synaxis (or assembly) of the Theotokos, written by Saint Romanos the Hymnographer.

28

Gold, Frankincense, and Myrrh

The adoration of Jesus by the wise men from the East is part of the Nativity celebration in the Orthodox Church.[1] Whatever the actual historical circumstances of the event—and Orthodox tradition takes them quite literally—the spiritual and theological significance of the coming of the kings with their gifts is of paramount importance.

We have already seen how the Church emphasizes the fact that the entire order of nature participates in the announcement of Christ's birth, thus revealing itself as God's creation. For, as the troparion of the feast proclaims, "those who worshipped the stars were taught by a star" to adore Jesus as Lord.

The riddles of the soothsayers
And the diviner Balaam are now fulfilled.
For a star has dawned from Jacob,
Leading the Magi, Persian kings bringing gifts,
To the Sun of Glory.

The error of Persia has ceased,
For the stargazers, kings of the East,
Bring gifts to Christ the King of all at His birth:
Gold, frankincense, and myrrh.
Bless Him, O children, and praise Him, O priests,
Exalt Him, O people, throughout the ages.[2]

[1]In the Christian West the festival of the Epiphany is the Twelfth Day of Christmas and centers on the adoration of the Magi. In the East, the Epiphany feast centers on Christ's baptism in the Jordan.

[2]Compline of the final day of the prefeast of the Nativity, December 24.

The coming of the wise men also bears witness to the fact that Jesus has come as King and Lord for all people, and not only the Jews. In the persons of the Persian kings the Church sees all the peoples of the earth and all the kingdoms of men.

> The daughter of Babylon
> Once led David's children captive from Zion,
> Whom she had taken with the sword.
> But now she sends her own children,
> The Magi bearing gifts,
> To beg the Daughter of David in whom God came
>   to dwell.
> Therefore let us raise up the song:
> Let the whole creation bless the Lord,
> And exalt Him above all forever.[3]

> The Magi, kings of Persia,
> Knew that You, the Heavenly King,
> Were truly born on earth.
> They came to Bethlehem
> Led by the light of a star,
> And offered their chosen gifts:
> Gold, frankincense, and myrrh.
> Falling before You they worshipped,
> For they saw You who are timeless
> Lying as a babe in the cave.[4]

> Earth spreads out its wide spaces
> And receives the Creator,
> As He receives glory from angels
> And the star from the heavens,
> Gifts from the Magi
> And recognition from the whole world.[5]

The gifts of the Magi are of particular significance. They

---

[3]Matins of the feast of the Nativity.
[4]Compline of the Feast of the Nativity.
[5]Compline of the final day of the prefeast of the Nativity, December 24.

are interpreted symbolically in the liturgy of the feast. The gift of gold is taken as the sign that Jesus is the king of Israel, of the entire universe, and of the kingdom of God to come. This is a crucial part of the Christmas story in the gospels. It caused Herod to kill all the "male children in Bethlehem and in all the region who were two years old or under, according to the time which he had ascertained from the wise men" (Mt 2:16).

> Now when Jesus was born in Bethlehem of Judea in the days of Herod the king, behold, wise men from the East came to Jerusalem, saying, "Where is He who has been born king of the Jews? For we have seen His star in the East, and have come to worship Him." When Herod the king heard this, he was troubled, and all Jerusalem with him; and assembling all the chief priests and scribes of the people, he inquired of them where the Christ was to be born. They told him, "In Bethlehem of Judea; for so it is written by the prophet: 'And you, O Bethlehem, in the land of Judah, are by no means least among the rulers of Judah; for from you shall come a ruler who will govern My people Israel.' " (Mt 2:1-6)

The gift of frankincense is taken by the liturgy to signify the fact that Jesus is God, since incense is for worship, and only God may be worshipped.

And the gift of myrrh is for the Lord Jesus who has come to die as the perfect sacrifice for the people. For the dead were anointed with myrrh, as Jesus Himself was anointed, according to the scriptures, at the time of His death (Jn 19:39-40).

In the gifts of the Magi, therefore, are contained all the mysteries of Christ's coming. They point to the purpose of His appearance on earth. He is the royal king, the Son of David, whose kingdom will have no end. He is the victim, the Lamb of God, who by His death takes away the sins of the world. And He is God Himself, the divine Son of the Father: "Light of Light, true God of true God; begotten, not made;

of one essence with the Father, by whom all things were made;
who for us men and for our salvation came down from
heaven . . ." as the Nicene Creed declares.

The contemplation of the wise men and their gifts is an
integral and lasting part of the Church's celebration of the
Lord's Winter Pascha.

The kings, the first first fruits of the gentiles,
Bring You gifts at Your birth in Bethlehem
From a mother who knew no travail.
With myrrh they point to Your death,
With gold, to Your royal power,
With frankincense to the preeminence of Your divinity.[6]

When the Lord Jesus was born in Bethlehem of Judah,
Magi coming from the East
Worshipped God made man.
And eagerly opening their treasures,
They offered Him precious gifts:
Refined gold, as to the King of the ages;
Frankincense, as to the God of all;
Myrrh they offered to the Immortal One
As one three days dead.
Come all nations, let us worship Him
Who was born to save our souls.[7]

[6]Compline of the final day of the prefeast of the Nativity, December 24.
[7]Compline of the feast of the Nativity.

29

The Blood of the Martyrs

The second day of Christmas in the Orthodox Church is dedicated to the Virgin Mary. It is called the synaxis of the Most Holy Theotokos. The Church assembles on this day to honor her through whom the Savior has come. The entire creation is indebted to the Lord for its redemption, but the Lord Himself is indebted to Mary who, humanly speaking, by the grace of the Spirit, made possible His coming.[1]

There then follow the three days of the postfeast of the Nativity dedicated to the memory of those who were killed for Christ. First is celebrated the memory of the first Christian martyr, the deacon Stephen. As the hymns of his festival declare, the persecution and death of Christians is an inevitable result of the coming of Christ. Jesus came to die for the truth of God, which is most perfectly actualized in the gift of one's life that others may live. This is the most godlike expression of love possible to creatures. Christ's disciples imitate His example, which is their calling and command, finding within it their highest joy and fulfillment.

A new commandment I give to you, that you love one another; even as I have loved you, that you also love one another. By this all men will know that you are My disciples, if you have love for one another. (Jn 13:34-35)

As the Father has loved Me, so have I loved you; abide

[1]This bold affirmation of Mary's free response and her voluntary collaboration in Christ's birth is repeated in many different ways by the Fathers of the Church.

in My love. If you keep My commandments, you will abide in My love, just as I have kept My Father's commandments and abide in His love. These things I have spoken to you, that My joy may be in you, and that your joy may be full. This is My commandment, that you love one another as I have loved you. Greater love has no man than this, that a man lay down his life for his friends. You are My friends if you do what I command you. (Jn 15:9-14)

More than all others, the martyrs are the friends of Christ. In their sufferings, according to the daring words of Saint Paul, they "complete what is lacking in Christ's afflictions for the sake of His body, that is the Church" (Col 1:24). This is certainly true in the case of Saint Stephen, whose martyr's death is recorded in detail in Saint Luke's Acts of the Apostles (see Acts 6-7).

> To the King and Lord of all
> Who is born on earth,
> The most beautiful Stephen is offered today,
> Adorned in the crimson of his own blood
> As with precious gems.
> Come, O lovers of the martyrs!
> Weave the flowers of song into a crown,
> Honoring the protomartyr of Christ our God
> For his spirit is radiant with wisdom and love.
> Through his prayers we receive peace and great mercy.[2]

> Yesterday the Master assumed our flesh
> And became our guest.
> Today His servant is stoned to death
> And departs in the flesh:
> The glorious protomartyr Stephen.[3]

Stephen is offered to the King

---

[2]Vespers of the feast of Saint Stephen. The word "stephan" in Greek means "crown."

[3]Kontakion of the feast of Saint Stephen.

As a living sacrifice.
For today he departs in the flesh
To God Almighty who came to dwell in the flesh,
Completing his combat in honor
For the sake of Christ.[4]

The third day of Christmas is dedicated to the memory of
the holy martyrs of Nicomedia who refused to honor the
earthly emperor as king in fidelity to the only King of heaven.
Their blood also, according to the ancient Christian saying,
has become the seed of the Church.

The throng of twenty thousand martyrs
Appears as a star in the Church,
For these noble men and women
Were inflamed with divine love for their Master,
And in the fire completed the course of their lives
In holiness and joy.[5]

Finally, on the fourth day of the feast, the "pascha" of
the innocent children slain by Herod is celebrated with praise.

Then Herod, when he saw that he had been tricked
by the wise men, was in a furious rage, and he sent
and killed all the male children in Bethlehem and in
all that region who were two years old or under, according to the time which he had ascertained from the
wise men. Then was fulfilled what was spoken by the
prophet Jeremiah: "A voice was heard in Ramah,
wailing and loud lamentation, Rachel weeping for her
children; she refused to be consoled, because they were
no more." (Mt 2:16-18)

Jesus escaped the slaughter of the children by his parents'
flight into Egypt. The angel warned Joseph in a dream, "Rise,
take the Child and His mother, and flee into Egypt, and
remain there till I tell you; for Herod is about to search for

---

[4]The hymn of light sung at matins of the feast of Saint Stephen.
[5]Kontakion of the feast of the Holy Martyrs of Nicomedia.

the Child, to destroy Him" (Mt 2:13). From His very first days Jesus was rejected on earth. He was hunted down by Herod, only to be finally caught by Pilate who, together with the leaders of His own people, put the Messiah to death. The reason for such hostility to the point of murder is given by Christ Himself when He says that "the light has come into the world, and men loved darkness rather than light, because their deeds were evil" (Jn 3:19).

Jesus' flight into Egypt is seen by the evangelist as fulfilling the prophetic words, "Out of Egypt have I called My Son" (Mt 2:15; Hos 11:1). He also sees Jesus' settlement in Nazareth as necessary to fulfill the words, "He shall be called a Nazarene" (Mt 2:23.) Egypt stands symbolically for the archenemy of Isarel, thus showing how "His own people received Him not" (Jn 1:11). And Nazareth stands for "Galilee of the Gentiles," again indicating the fact that the Messiah has come for all peoples.

The question put to all who celebrate Christ's Winter Pascha concerns their own relationship to the Lord. Are we ready to receive Him, and therefore to love as He has loved us, even to the point of death? Or are we among those who receive Him not, numbered with those who murder Him through our hatred and neglect of our neighbors? As Christ's beloved disciple has said, "He who says he is in the light and hates his brother is in the darkness still. . . . Anyone who hates his brother is a murderer, and you know that no murdered has eternal life abiding in him. By this we know love, that He laid down His life for us; and we ought to lay down our lives for the brethren" (1 Jn 2:9; 3:15-16).

> When Jesus was born in Bethlehem of Judah,
> The sceptre of the house of Judah passed away.
> Infants who leaped in play were slaughtered for Christ.
> A voice was heard in Ramah,
> The lamentation of Judah's daughters,
> Rachel weeping for her sons, as it is written
> For the lawless Herod murdered the infants.
> The land of Judah was soaked with innocent blood;
> The earth was reddened by the blood of babies.

But the Church of the Gentiles is washed by this blood;
Clothed in radiant purity, she cries in joy:
The Truth has come!
God is made manifest!
He is born of the Virgin,
Enlightening those who sit in darkness,
For the salvation of the world![6]

---

[6]Vespers of the feast of the Holy Innocents.

30

The Circumcision of the Lord

On the eighth day of the feast of the Nativity, which also happens to be the first day of the civil new year, the Church celebrates the Lord's circumcision and His receiving the name Jesus, which means Savior.

> And at the end of eight days, when He was circumcised,
> He was called Jesus, the name given by the angel before
> He was conceived in the womb. (Lk 2:21)

This day is also the anniversary of the death of Saint Basil the Great, whose memory is part of the liturgical feast.

> The Lord of all accepts to be circumcised;
> Thus in His mercy He circumcises the sins of mortal men.
> Today He grants the world salvation,
> While Basil, high priest of God our Creator,
> Rejoices in heaven as the radiant star of the Church.[1]

According to the Church's liturgy, the Lord underwent circumcision in order to fulfill the law of Moses, which no one had been able to fulfill before. In performing "everything according to the law" (Lk 2:39), the Messiah finds it fitting "to fulfill all righteousness" (Mt 3:15). In this sense He is the fulfillment of the law and the prophets; not only by doing what was written of Him, but also by doing all things that everyone should do if they truly fulfilled the Word of God.

---

[1]Kontakion of the feast of the Lord's Circumcision and Saint Basil the Great.

The God of all goodness
Did not disdain to be circumcised.
He offered Himself as a saving sign
And example for us all.
He fulfilled the words of the prophets concerning Himself.
He holds the world in His hands,
Yet is bound in swaddling clothes.
Let us glorify Him![2]

In performing everything exactly according to the law, the Lord shows that He has come to be a servant, and to identify Himself completely with His sinful creatures. This is God's divine humility, His exceedingly great lovingkindness and compassion, His ineffable and unspeakable humiliation and condescension to us who are lost. For He not only is found "in the likeness of men," but He empties Himself of His divine glory, and takes on the "form of a slave" (Phil 2:7-8), He submits to the high priest's knife, enduring the sign of complete submission to God, the act which expresses the total helplessness and weakness of unholy creatures before their Holy Creator. Words cannot convey the condescension of the Lord in His willingness to be circumcised. It is an act of self-emptying humiliation which is wholly ineffable.

Enthroned on high with the Eternal Father and
    Your Divine Spirit,
You willed to be born on earth, O Jesus,
From the unwedded handmaiden, Your mother.
Therefore You were circumcised as an eight-day child.
Glory to Your most gracious counsel!
Glory to Your dispensation!
Glory to Your condescension,
O only Lover of man![3]

In allowing Himself to be circumcised, the Lord delivers His people from the curse of the law and frees them from the ritual signs of the covenant based on law. The law of God is

[2]Vespers of the feast of the Lord's Circumcision.
[3]Troparion of the feast of the Lord's Circumcision.

not itself a curse, although some Christian theologies appear
to teach this. The apostle Paul says that "the law is holy,
and the commandment is holy and just and good" (Rom
7:12). The problem is that no one can keep the law. If we
were to be judged by the works of the law, all would perish.
For this reason the Messiah comes, to do in mortal flesh that
which no one else could do, so that by faith in Him all who
believe may be made righteous before God.

Circumcision itself was given in response to faith. It was
the sign of belonging faithfully to the Lord. Even in its
original form and meaning, it was not something merely
physical, but spiritual; a matter not simply of the flesh, but
of the heart.

> Circumcision indeed is of value if you obey the law;
> but if you break the law, your circumcision becomes
> uncircumcision. So, if a man who is uncircumcised
> keeps the precepts of the law, will not his uncircum-
> cision be regarded as circumcision? Then those who
> are physically uncircumcised but keep the law will
> condemn you who have the written code and circum-
> cision but break the law. For he is not a real Jew who
> is one outwardly, nor is true circumcision something
> external and physical. He is a Jew who is one inwardly,
> and real circumcision is a matter of the heart, spiritual
> and not literal. His praise is not from men but from
> God. (Rom 2:25-29)

Because of His total righteousness, ritualistic and moral,
physical and spiritual, legal and ethical, Jesus the Messiah
liberates His people from everything that belongs to this
world and opens to them the life of the coming age of God's
kingdom. "For in Christ Jesus neither circumcision nor uncircumcision is of any avail, but faith working through love"
(Gal 5:6).

> Was any one at the time of his call already circum-
> cised? Let him not seek to remove the marks of cir-
> cumcision. Was any one at the time of his call un-

circumcised? Let him not seek circumcision. For neither
circumcision counts for anything nor uncircumcision,
but keeping the commandments of God. (1 Cor 7:18-
19)

It is those who want to make a good showing in the
flesh that would compel you to be circumcised, and only
in order that they may not be persecuted for the cross
of Christ. For even those who receive circumcision do
not themselves keep the law, but they desire to have
you circumcised that they may glory in your flesh. But
far be it from me to glory except in the cross of our
Lord Jesus Christ, by which the world has been crucified to me, and I to the world. For neither circumcision counts for anything, nor uncircumcision, but a
new creation. (Gal 6:12-15)

In celebrating the Winter Pascha, the faithful come to
know for themselves that truly "if any one is in Christ, he
is a new creation; the old has passed away, behold, the new
has come" (2 Cor 5:17).

Circumcision has ceased,
For Christ was circumcised of His own will,
Granting the nations remission of sins,
And saving them by grace.

The eighth day,
The day on which Christ the Master was circumcised in
    the flesh,
Portrays the eternal life of the age to come.

He who without separation and corruption
Was born ineffably as the Word of the Father,
Who is God from God in the changeless Godhead,
Undergoes circumcision in the flesh.
He who is above the law
Delivers all from the curse of the law
By becoming Himself under the law

And giving us blessings from on high.
Therefore we praise His infinitely gracious condescension,
We sing His praises,
And we glorify Him with thanksgiving,
Entreating Him that our souls may be saved.[4]

[4]Matins of the feast of the Lord's Circumcision. The reference to the "eighth day" as "portraying the eternal life of the age to come" is repeated in several different ways in the hymns of the feast. This comes from the Jewish and early Christian teaching that the Day of the Lord, which is the Day of God's kingdom, is beyond the time of this world which is measured in weeks of seven days. Thus the "day after the Sabbath," the "eighth day," symbolizes the age to come. The fact that circumcision and naming took place on this day is therefore a symbol of eternal life. It is for this reason also that most of the Church's major festivals are celebrated in "octaves," that is, for a period of eight days.

31

The Lord's Epiphany in the Jordan

Like the liturgical celebration of the Lord's Nativity, the festival of His Epiphany in the Jordan at the time of His baptism is inaugerated with a prefeast celebration of five days. And also like the services of the Nativity, many hymns of the Epiphany prefeast are patterned after those of the springtime Pascha of the Lord's death and resurrection. Once again just a few words in many of the songs are changed from those sung during Holy Week in order to glorify the present mystery.

Come, O faithful,
Having enjoyed the Master's hospitality,
The Banquet of Immortality in the lowly manger,
Let us run to the Jordan,
There to see a strange mystery,
Revealing the Light from on high.[1]

The feast of Christ's Birth has passed;
It shone more brightly than the sun.
The day of His Epiphany is coming;
That day will be even more radiant.
There the shepherds gave glory with angels,
Worshipping God made man.
Here John's right hand will touch the Master
As he cries out in fear:
Sanctify both me and the waters,
O Only Merciful One![2]

[1]Compline of the third day of the prefeast of the Epiphany, January 4.
[2]Matins of the first day of the prefeast of the Epiphany, January 2.

The feast which passed was radiant,
But the coming one is even more glorious!
There the Magi worshipped the Savior;
Here the servant baptizes the Master.
There the shepherds saw the Child and were amazed;
Here the voice of the Father proclaims the only-
     begotten Son![3]

As we have seen, the word "epiphany" means "manifestation" or "appearance." It is used for the event of Christ's
baptism because it was in the Jordan, being baptized by John
the Forerunner, that Jesus appeared to the world and manifested Himself as the Messiah, the Son of God, one of the
Holy Trinity.

The Lord's first public appearance takes place at His baptism for very good reason. Baptism is the symbol of death
and resurrection; Christ came to the earth in order to die
and be raised. Baptism is a symbol of repentance of sin, and
its forgiveness; Christ came as the Lamb of God who takes
upon Himself the sin of the world in order to take it away.
Baptism is a symbol of sanctification; Christ has come to
sanctify the whole of creation. Baptism is a symbol, finally, of
radical renewal. When one is baptized the old is over and the
new has come. And Christ has appeared on earth to bring all
things to an end, and to make all things new. The act of
baptism, therefore, contains in symbol the entire mystery of
Christ, the whole purpose of His coming.

Christ did not need to be baptized for Himself. This is
made perfectly clear in the gospels. He had to be baptized
for our sake, in order "to fulfill all righteousness" (Mt 3:15).

Then Jesus came from Galilee to the Jordan to John,
to be baptized by him. John would have prevented
Him, saying, "I need to be baptized by You, and do
You come to me?" But Jesus answered him, "Let it
be so now; for thus it is fitting for us to fulfill all
righteousness." Then he consented. And when Jesus
was baptized, He went up immediately from the water

[3]Vespers of the third day of the prefeast of the Epiphany, January 4.

and behold, the heavens were opened and He saw the Spirit of God descending like a dove, and alighting on Him; and lo, a voice from heaven, saying, "This is My beloved Son, with whom I am well pleased." (Mt 3:13-17)

The baptism of John was a "baptism of repentance for the forgiveness of sins." The people came to John for baptism "confessing their sins" (Mk 1:4-5). The Lord Jesus had no need of repentance. As God's Son in human flesh He committed no sin. His baptism, therefore, manifests His complete identification with His sinful creatures. He literally becomes one of us, not only in our humanity, but in our sinfulness; not only in our life on earth, but also in our death. For as the apostle Paul has written, "For our sake He [God the Father] made Him to be sin who knew no sin, so that in Him we might become the righteousness of God" (2 Cor 5:21).

But we see Jesus, who for a little while was made lower than the angels, crowned with glory and honor because of the suffering of death, so that by the grace of God He might taste death for every one. . . . Since therefore the children share in flesh and blood, He Himself likewise partook of the same nature, that through death He might destroy him who has the power of death, that is, the devil, and deliver all those who through fear of death were subject to lifelong bondage. . . . Therefore He had to be made like His brethren in every respect, so that He might become a merciful and faithful high priest in the service of God, to make expiation for the sins of the people. (Heb 2:9, 14-15, 17)

In the Church's celebration of the Lord's Epiphany in the Jordan, the faithful are enabled to see Jesus made like them in every respect, entering the waters to identify with their fallen condition in order to bring it to an end and to create them anew for life in the kingdom of God. They become

convinced through this liturgical experience that He is indeed
the Christ, the Son of the Living God, who has come to save
the world.

> Let us assemble in spirit, O faithful,
> At the streams of the Jordan
> That we may behold a great and mighty wonder.
> We shall see the Creator of all made manifest
> As He comes to be baptized.[4]
> Let us pass, O faithful,
> From Bethlehem to Jordan.
> For behold, the Light which came into the darkness,
> There begins to overcome the night.[5]

> Let us, the guests of God's banquet,
> Who feasted in Bethlehem,
> Giving glory to the incarnate Lord with the angels, wise
>   men, and shepherds,
> Now proceed in the spirit to the Jordan
> To see Christ perform a great mystery.
> Let us exalt Him throughout all ages.[6]

> Your coming in the flesh, O Christ,
> Fulfilled the law
> And accomplished the first act of salvation.
> Now in Your compassion You come to the Jordan;
> Your head is bowed to the Baptist
> And the completion of Your work is begun.
> Cry out in faith, O people:
> Blessed is our God made manifest!
> Glory to You![7]

---

[4]Vespers of the second day of the prefeast of the Epiphany, January 3.
[5]Matins of the second day of the prefeast of the Epiphany, January 3.
[6]Compline of the third day of the prefeast of the Epiphany, January 4.
[7]Matins of the second day of the prefeast of the Epiphany, January 3.

32

The Manifestation of the Trinity

Jesus' baptism in the Jordan, which contains all the mysteries of our salvation, is not only His epiphany as the Messiah, the Suffering Servant of the Lord. It is also the first manifestation to the world of the greatest mystery of all, the worship of the Holy Trinity.

Let streams of tears exhaust our eyes,
Let us cleanse the filth of our souls, O believers!
We shall see Christ,
The Light from the Three-fold Light,
Coming to be baptized.
The Father will bear witness from heaven,
And the Holy Spirit will come in the form of a
    shining dove.[1]

When You, O Lord, were baptized in the Jordan,
The worship of the Trinity was made manifest.
For the voice of the Father bare witness to You,
And called You His beloved Son.
And the Spirit, in the form of a dove,
Confirmed the truthfulness of His word.
O Christ our God, who has revealed Yourself
And has enlightened the world,
Glory to You![2]

At Jesus' baptism the mystery of all mysteries is clearly revealed to the world for the very first time. It is the open

[1]Compline of the second day of the prefeast of the Epiphany, January 3.
[2]Troparion of the feast of the Epiphany.

revelation, hinted at dimly in the "shadows" of the previous covenants of Israel, that the one true God is essentially a Father.[3] Being Love itself, God cannot remain isolated in the perfection of His divinity. This, we are told in the events of God's "final and everlasting covenant," sealed by the divine blood of the Messiah, would be a contradiction in terms. The absolutely perfect God who is Love itself—"for God is love" (1 Jn 4:8, 16)—must be self-sharing by nature. He must manifest Himself and His divine perfection in the divine person of Another. And He does. For He has a Son who is eternal, divine, and uncreated; a Son who is His divine Image and Word[4]; a Son who is "the Radiance of the glory of God and the Express Image of His Person" (Heb 1:3).[5] This is His beloved Son, or, in the more exact expression of the apostle Paul, the "Son of His Love" (Col 1:13).[6] All things were created by and for this Son.[7] "He is before all things, and in Him all things hold together" (Col 1:17).[8] But "though He was in the form of God, [He] did not count equality with God a thing to be grasped, but emptied Himself, taking the form of a slave, being born in the likeness of men" (Phil 2:6-7.)

> And being found in human form He humbled Himself and became obedient unto death, even death on a cross. Therefore God has highly exalted Him and bestowed on Him the name which is above every name, that at the name of Jesus every knee should bow, in heaven and on earth and under the earth, and every tongue confess that Jesus Christ is Lord, to the glory of God the Father. (Phil 2:8-11)

[3]The apostolic writings of the first Christians use the distinction between "shadow" and "reality" to describe the relationship between the two covenants; see Col 2:17 and Heb 10:1.

[4]Jn 1:1-18; Col 1:15; 2 Cor 4:4. See above, pp. 12-14.

[5]See above, p. 14, n. 4.

[6]The Revised Standard Version translates this as "beloved Son"; literally, the text says "the Son of His love."

[7]Jn 1:1-3; Heb 1:1-3; Col 1:16.

[8]John the Baptist himself testifies that Jesus was before him (Jn 1:30). And Jesus claims that even "before Abraham was, I AM" (Jn 8:58).

With the manifestation of God's Son as Jesus the Christ of Israel and the Savior of the world, God's Holy Spirit is also manifested as a unique divine person. He too was dimly prefigured in His activities in the old covenants, but is now revealed in His personal glory. He is the "Spirit of Truth, who proceeds from the Father" (Jn 15:26). He descends personally on the man Jesus, anointing Him in His humanity, and all people in Him, showing Him to the world as the promised Messiah, and shining forth from Him upon all who receive Him as their Lord and God.[9]

This is the unique doctrine of orthodox Christianity: the worship of the Divine Trinity "one in essence and undivided."[10] It was foreshadowed in the theophanies of the Old Covenant of Israel. It was approached in the contemplations of the holy people of various "world religions." It was obscurely discovered in the speculations of the mystical philosophers of all nations, especially the Greeks. And it was clearly made manifest in the "final and everlasting covenant of peace" of the one true God with His people, first revealed in the Messiah's epiphany at His baptism in the Jordan. This worship stands at the heart of the celebration of the Winter Pascha in the Orthodox Church.

Seeing You, O Christ our God,
Drawing near to him in the river Jordan,
John said: Why are You who are without defilement
Come to Your servant, O Lord?
In whose name shall I baptize You?
Of the Father? But You bear Him in Yourself.
Of the Son? But You are Yourself the Son made flesh.
Of the Holy Spirit? But You know that from Your
    own lips You give Him to the faithful.
O God who has appeared, have mercy on us![11]

[9]See Jn 1:33-34; 15:26; 16:7-15; 20:28.

[10]This is a liturgical formula from the divine liturgy of Saint John Chrysostom.

[11]Compline of the feast of the Epiphany; also sung at vespers of the second day of the postfeast.

The Trinity was made manifest in the Jordan,
For the Father, supreme in divinity, bore witness saying,
He who is here baptized is My beloved Son;
And the Spirit, equal in divinity, rested upon Him,
Whom the people bless and exalt above all forever.

Come, O faithful,
Let us speak of things divine,
Joining the angels in unending hymns
To glorify the God in whom we have received initiation:
Father, Son, and Holy Spirit,
The Trinity, consubstantial in Persons,
Yet one God to whom we sing:
Blessed are You, O God of our fathers![12]

---

[12]Matins of the feast of the Epiphany.

33

The River Jordan

The river Jordan plays a very important role in the Bible. Before it becomes the river in which Jesus the Messiah is baptized, it is revealed as the river which bounds the "promised land." To cross the Jordan, for the people of Israel, was to enter into the fulfillment of the Lord's promises. It was to enter into the "land flowing with milk and honey," the place where God would dwell with His people providing them with the endless blessings of His presence.

In the New Testament, with its spiritual and mystical fulfillment of the Old, to cross the Jordan was to enter into the Kingdom of God, to experience the fulness of the life of the age to come. The fact that Moses was not blessed to cross the Jordan thus became a symbol of the fact that the Law by itself could not save Israel or the world. It had to be Joshua, which literally means *Savior,* and is the Hebrew form of the Greek word *Jesus,* who leads the people across the Jordan and into the promised land, thus symbolizing the saving action of the new Joshua, Jesus the messianic Savior, in the covenant of grace.

> After the death of Moses the servant of the Lord, the Lord said to Joshua the son of Nun, Moses' minister, "Moses my servant is dead; now therefore arise, go over this Jordan, you and all this people, into the land which I am giving to them, to the people of Israel." (Josh 1:1-2)

When Joshua came to the Jordan the streams parted at the presence of God's People, with the priests bearing in their

hands the Ark of the Covenant. As the waters of the sea
parted to allow God's people to pass through as if on dry
land at their exodus from Egypt, so also at the entry into the
land of promise the river Jordan made way for God's people
to pass through into the place of their final destination.

> Behold the ark of the covenant of the Lord of all
> the earth is to pass over before you into the Jordan.
> Now therefore take twelve men from the tribes of
> Isarel, from each tribe a man. And when the soles
> of the feet of the priests who bear the ark of the Lord,
> the Lord of all the earth, shall rest in the waters of the
> Jordan, the waters of the Jordan shall be stopped from
> flowing, and the waters coming down from above shall
> stand in one heap." (Josh 3:11-13)

The Lord also commanded Joshua to take twelve stones out
of the river Jordan and to place them together in one place
in a pile where the people had passed through, to remain "to
the people of Isarel a memorial forever" of the what the
Lord had done for them.

> And the men of Israel did as Joshua commanded, and
> took up twelve stones out of the midst of the Jordan,
> according to the number of the tribes of the people of
> Israel, as the Lord told Joshua, and they carried them
> over with them to the place where they lodged, and
> laid them down there. And Joshua set up twelve stones
> in the midst of the Jordan, in the place where the feet
> of the priests bearing the ark of the covenant had
> stood; and they are there to this day. For the priests
> who bore the ark stood in the midst of the Jordan,
> until everything was finished that the Lord com-
> manded Joshua to tell the people, according to all that
> Moses had commanded Joshua. (Josh 4:8-10)

After the people passed through the Jordan river, "the waters
of the Jordan returned to their place and overflowed all its
banks, as before." (Josh 4:18) This miraculous wonder

became part of the living memory of Israel, and the event was celebrated in the worship of God's people ever since. The psalms which recall this divine action are sung at the Church's festival of the Epiphany as prefigurations of God's final act of the salvation of all people in the death and resurrection of His Anointed, the Beloved Son who was baptized in the same Jordan streams.

> When Israel went forth from Egypt,
>> the house of Jacob from a people of strange language.
> Judah became his sanctuary,
>> Israel his dominion.
> The sea looked and fled,
>> Jordan turned back.
> The mountains skipped like rams,
>> the hills like lambs.
> What ails you, O sea, that you flee?
>> O Jordan, that you turn back?
> O mountains, that you skip like rams?
>> O hills, like lambs?
> Tremble, O earth, at the presence of the Lord,
>> at the presence of the God of Jacob,
> who turns the rock into a pool of water,
>> the flint into a spring of water. (Ps 114)

The river Jordan was also parted by the passage of Elijah and Elisha, an event also recalled at the liturgy of Epiphany. (2 Kings 2) And it was from the Jordan that Elijah was taken up into heaven in order to return again, as the tradition developed, to prepare the way for the coming of the Messiah. (See Mt 17:9-13) It was also in the Jordan that Naaman the Syrian was cleansed from his leprosy, a sign referred to by Jesus as a prefiguration of the salvation of all people, not only those of Israel. (Lk 4:27) In the account of Naaman's cure the special significance of the Jordan is stressed once again.

> And Elisha sent a messenger to him saying, "Go and wash in the Jordan seven times, and your flesh shall

be restored, and you shall be clean." But Naaman was angry and went away, saying , "Behold, I thought that he would surely come out to me, and stand, and call on the name of the Lord his God, and wave his hand over the place, and cure the leper. Are not Abana and Pharpar, the rivers of Damascus better than all the waters of Israel? Could I not wash in them and be clean? So he turned and went away in rage. But his servants came near and said to him, "My father, if the prophet commanded you to do some great thing, would you not have done it? How much rather, then, when he says to you, 'Wash, and be clean'?" So he went down and dipped himself seven times in the Jordan, according to the word of the man of God; and his flesh was restored like the flesh of a little child, and he was clean. (2 Kings 5:10-14)

Can we not be washed in just any river and be clean? God's answer is, No. Only in the Jordan, in the baptism of Christ, are we cleansed from all of our sins. Only through the Jordan do we enter into the land of the living, the promised land of God's kingdom. Only by the sanctified waters of the Jordan does God sanctify us forever.

> The River Jordan turned back of old,
> Before Elisha's mantle when Elijah ascended.
> The waters were made to part in two,
> So the wet surface became a dry path.
> This was in truth a symbol of baptism
> By which we pass through mortal life.
> Christ has come to the Jordan to sanctify the waters.[1]

> Seeing you, the Creator, naked in the waters,
> Asking to be baptized,
> The whole order of creation was struck with confusion
>   and fear.
> The Forerunner was paralyzed and dared not
> approach You.

[1]Troparion of the prefeast of the Epiphany.

The sea fled and the Jordan was driven back.
The mountains skipped like lambs beholding You.
The hosts of angels surrounding You cried out:
O Wonder! The Savior is stripped naked,
In His desire to clothe, to save and to refashion Man.[2]

Joshua the son of Nun
Led the people and the ark into the river Jordan
Foreshadowing the goodness which was to come.
Their passage was an image of our regeneration,
A sure type of the new creation accomplished by the Spirit,
To sanctify the waters.[3]

The hand of the Baptist trembled,
When he touched Your most pure head.
The river Jordan turned back,
Not daring to minister to You.
For how could that river which stood in awe of Joshua,
    the son of Nun,
Not be afraid before Joshua's Creator?
But You, O Savior, have fulfilled all that was appointed,
That You might save the world by Your Epiphany,
O Only Lover of Man![4]

[2]Vespers of the postfeast of the Epiphany.
[3]Matins of the postfeast of the Epiphany.
[4]Vespers of the feast of the Epiphany.

34

The Great Blessing of Water

The rite of the Great Blessing of Water is celebrated in the Orthodox Church after the vesperal divine liturgy on the eve of the feast of the Epiphany, and after the eucharistic liturgy on the day itself.[1] It begins with the chanting of special hymns with the incensing of the water, and concludes with bible readings, petitions and prayers.[2]

The voice of the Lord upon the waters cries out saying:
Come, receive ye all the Spirit of wisdom,
The Spirit of understanding, the Spirit of the fear of God,
The Spirit of Christ who is made manifest.

Today the nature of the waters is sanctified,
The Jordan bursts forth and turns back the
     flood of its streams,
Seeing the Master wash himself.

As a man You came to that river, O Christ the King,
Hastening to receive the baptism of a servant,
At the hands of the Forerunner because of our sins,
O Good One who loves Mankind.

[1]The usual practice in parish churches is to bless the water just once, at the time when most people can be present. According to most *Typika*, the water should be blessed in a receptacle inside the church building on the eve of the feast, and outside in a natural setting on the day itself. This is done in churches where it can be easily accomplished.

[2]The scripture readings at the Great Blessing of Water are from Isaiah: 1. 35:1-10. 2. 55:1-13. 3. 12:3-6. The Psalm verses are taken from Psalm 114 and Psalm 28. The Epistle reading is 1 Corinthians 10:1-4. The Gospel reading is the baptism of Jesus according to the Gospel of St. Mark.

To the voice of one crying in the wilderness,
Prepare ye the way of the Lord,
You came, O Lord, taking the form of a servant,
Asking for baptism though You have no sin.
The waters saw You and were afraid.
The Forerunner began to tremble and cried out, saying:
How shall the lampstand illumine the Light?
How shall the servant lay hands upon the Master?
Sanctify both me and the waters, O Savior,
Who takes away the sins of the world.[3]

The water placed in a large receptacle in the midst of the church, or freely flowing in a natural source, is decorated with candles and flowers as the symbol of the beautiful world of God's original creation through His Word and Spirit—the same beautiful world which shall become the Kingdom of God at the end of the ages through its redemption by the Word Incarnate, Jesus Christ, and the same Holy Spirit.

People sometimes think that the blessing of water, and the practice of drinking it and sprinkling it on people and things, is a "paganism" which has crept into the Christian Church. We know, however, that this ritual was practiced by the People of God before the coming of Christ, as well as at the time of His manifestation. (See John 5-7) And we know that it has existed among Christians from very early times, being witnessed from the beginning especially in connection with the practice of baptism.

The service of the Great Blessing of Water itself reveals the action's meaning for the Christian people. The readings from the Bible, particularly the messianic words from the prophecy of Isaiah, together with the prayers, petitions and hymns all serve to manifest the meaning of the great festival of the Manifestation of the Messiah.

Thus says the Lord, The wilderness and the solitary place shall be glad for them; and the desert shall rejoice and blossom as the rose. It shall blossom abundantly and rejoice even with joy and singing . . . they

[3]Opening hymns from the rite of the Great Blessing of Water.

shall see the glory of the Lord and the excellency of
our God . . . He will come and save you. Then the eyes
of the blind shall be opened, and the ears of the deaf
shall be unstopped. Then shall the lame man leap as an
hart, and the tongue of the dumb sing: for in the
wilderness shall waters break out, and streams in the
desert. And the parched ground shall become a pool,
and the thirsty land springs of water. . . . (Is 35:1-10)

God has sent His only-begotten Son "not to condemn the
world, but that the world might be saved through him."
(Jn 3:17) He has sent the Lord Jesus Christ not only to save
people's souls, but to save their bodies, and not only to save
human beings, but to save the entire creation.

You are great, O Lord, and Your works are wondrous,
and there are no words capable of hymning your
wonders . . . For of Your own will You brought all
things into being from nothing, by Your power You
uphold the whole of creation, and by Your providence
You order the world . . . The sun sings to You, the
moon glorifies You, the stars meet together before
Your face, the light obeys You, the deeps shudder
before You, the water springs serve You . . . We
confess Your grace, we proclaim Your mercy, we
conceal not Your gracious acts: You have set free our
mortal nature. By Your birth You have sanctified the
virgin's womb. All creation sings praises to You Who
have revealed Yourself. For You, our God, have appeared upon earth and have dwelled among men. You
have sanctified the Jordan streams. . . . Therefore O
Master, be present here now by the descent of the
Holy Spirit, and sanctify this water. Give it the blessing
of Jordan. Make it a fountain of incorruption, a gift of
sanctification, a remission of sins, a protection against
disease, a destruction of demons . . . and may it be
for those who will partake of it, to the cleansing of
their souls and bodies, to the healing of their passions,

to the sanctification of their homes, to every expedient purpose. . . .[4]

Since the Son of God has taken human flesh and has appeared in the world, manifesting Himself in His baptism in the Jordan, all flesh and all matter is sanctified. Everything is made pure and holy in Him. Everything which is corrupted and polluted by the sinful works of men is cleansed and purified by the gracious works of God. All death-dealing powers of the devil which poison the good world of God's creation are destroyed. All things are again made new. Through the "prime element" of water on the feast of the Epiphany the entire creation is shown to be sanctified by God's Word through the same Spirit of God who "in the beginning . . . was moving over the face of the waters." (Gen 1:2)

Come, O ye faithful,
Let us praise the greatness of God's dispensation
    toward us,
For He who became Man because of our transgressions
And who alone is clean and undefiled,
Was for our cleansing Himself cleansed in the Jordan
That He might sanctify both me and the waters . . .
Let us then draw water in gladness, O Brothers,
For upon those that draw in faith
The grace of the Spirit is invisibly bestowed by Christ
The God and Savior of our souls.[5]

[4]The Main Prayer from the rite of the Great Blessing of Water.
[5]Concluding Hymn from the rite of the Great Blessing of Water.

35

The Grace of God has Appeared

The epistle readings for the liturgy of Epiphany and the Sunday following the festival deserve our careful attention and meditation. The reading for the feast is taken from Saint Paul's letter to Titus.

> For the grace of God has appeared for the salvation of all people, training us to renounce impiety and worldly passions, and to live sober, upright and godly lives in this world, awaiting our blessed hope, the appearing of the glory of our great God and Savior Jesus Christ, who gave himself for us to redeem us from all iniquity and to purify for himself a people of his own who are zealous for good deeds. (. . .) But when the goodness and loving kindness of God our Saviour appeared, he saved us, not because of deeds done by us in righteousness, but in virtue of his own mercy, by the washing of regeneration and renewal in the Holy Spirit, which he poured out upon us richly through Jesus Christ our Savior, so that we might be justified by his grace and become heirs of eternal life. (Titus 2:11-14; 3:4-7)

The word for *appearing* in this letter is the Greek word *epiphania.* And where the apostle uses the verb *to appear,* again the root word in Greek is *epiphanein.*

The grace of God, is said to make its epiphany for the salvation of all people. Divine grace shines forth so that something can happen in the lives of people while still living in this world. What happens is that we are to react to God's grace by specific works of conversion. We are to respond to God's grace by renouncing impiety and worldly passions which are our lustful cravings for ego-gratification and fleshly pleasures which inevitably lead us to hostility, anger, distress, frustration and depression. All this disappears when God's grace appears. What comes instead is sobriety and uprightness; dispassion, self-control, interior freedom and voluntary self-determination according to God's will. This is real liberation; the only genuine liberation that exists. All other "liberation" is in fact enslavement. For the grace of God liberates; the power of the devil, working through the ego and the flesh, enslaves.

When people respond to the grace of God that appears, the result is one of blessed hope; the happy expectation of another appearing, another *epiphania,* which is that of the final "glory of our great God and Savior Jesus Christ" which is to come at the end of the ages. In a word, the first appearing of Jesus to "redeem us from all inquity and to purify us for himself as a people zealous for good deeds" results directly in our anticipation of the ultimate resolution of all things in the Lord's second coming: the *epiphania* at the end.

Thus there are two epiphanies; two manifestations and appearances. The first is for our salvation and redemption which God has accomplished in Christ "not because of any deeds done by us in righteousness, but by virtue of his own mercy." And the second is when, being "justified (or made *righteous*) by his grace," we actually enter into the eternal life of God's kingdom. We participate in the second only on condition that we love the first; and prove our love by our godly lives fulfilled in good deeds.

The apostle Paul gives the same teaching in the letter ascribed to him to the Ephesians which is read at the liturgy on the Lord's Day following the Epiphany feast.

> But grace was given to each of us according to the measure of Christ's gift. Therefore it is said, "When he ascended on high he led a host of captives, and he gave gifts to men." In saying, "He ascended," what does it mean but that he had also descended into the

lower parts of the earth? He who descended is he who also ascended far above the heavens, that he might fill all things. And his gifts were that some should be apostles, some prophets, some evangelists, some pastors and teachers, to equip the saints for the work of ministry, for building up the body of Christ, until we all attain to the unity of faith of the knowledge of the Son of God, to mature personhood, to the measure of the stature of the fulness of Christ. (Eph 4:7-13)

In His baptism in the Jordan, and in His subsequent ministry, the Son of God descended into the human condition to the very depths so that He might fill all things with Himself. And after His descent, He ascended into the heavens, taking us with Him into the presence of God, and giving us gifts for the sake of service. Each person has a different gift and a different calling. Whatever it may be, it is given for the sake of building up the body of Christ, which is the Church; and for the sake of the sanctity and salvation of all. The goal of everyone is "mature personhood: the measure of the stature of the fulness of Christ."

Earlier in the same letter to the Ephesians the apostle insisted that being saved by grace through faith, the Christian people are Christ's workmanship made for good works with the ultimate goal being to "know the love of Christ which surpasses knowledge," and so to be "filled with all the fulness of God." This takes place within Christ's Church "which is His body, the fulness of Him who fills all in all." (Eph 1:23, 2:8-10, 3:19)

The grace of God has appeared for the salvation of all people. The salvation which God's grace brings in its appearance is that all people might do the good deeds that Christ Himself has done, and so attain unto the measure of the stature of His fulness, thus being filled with all the fulness of God. The apostle Paul sums this up for himself in his second letter to Timothy.

I have fought the good fight, I have finished the race, I have kept the faith. Henceforth there is laid up for

me the crown of righteousness which the Lord, the
righteous judge, will award to me on that Day, and
not only to me but also to all who have loved his
appearing—*epiphania.* (2 Tim 4:7-8)

If we love the Lord's epiphany, and prove it by our zeal
for good deeds, than we too shall receive our crowns from
Christ, the righteous judge, on the Day of His final appearing.

Christ our Salvation has appeared,
Granting enlightenment.
Let the heavens greatly rejoice,
And let the clouds pour down righteousness on
    those who cry:
Blessed are You, O God of our fathers.[1]

Come, let us purify our senses.
Let us behold the fulness of divine glory in the flesh.
Let us see Christ baptized, fighting the devil's deceit.
Let us sing praises to His sinless person:
Blessed is our God who has appeared!
Glory to You![2]

Come, O dwellers on the earth, harmfully led astray.
Let us purify our minds and our perceptions.
As we see Christ baptized in the flesh by the
    Forerunner John.
Let us all sing to Him, crying out with faith:
Blessed is our God who has appeared!
Glory to You![3]

Lifegiving riches spring up for us in the Jordan streams.
Baptismal grace by which we who are enlightened by
    the washing say:
Glory to You who enlightened the universe!
You give life to us who sing:
Blessed is our God who has appeared!
Glory to You![4]

[1]Matins of the prefeast of Epiphany.
[2]Vespers of the postfeast of Epiphany.
[3]Matins of the postfeast of Epiphany.
[4]Matins of the postfeast of Epiphany.

36

The Greatest Born of Woman

The second day of the feast of the Epiphany is called the Synaxis of Saint John, the prophet, forerunner and baptist of the Lord. It is a day of liturgical celebration in honor of the one who prepared the way for the Messiah and baptized Him in the Jordan river. According to Jesus himself, there is no one greater than John the Baptist.

> And this is the testimony of John, when the Jews sent priests and Levites from Jerusalem to ask him, "Who are you?" He confessed, he did not deny, but confessed, "I am not the Christ," And they asked him, "What then? Are you Elijah?" He said, "I am not." "Are you the prophet?" And he answered, "No." They said to him then, "Who are you? Let us have an answer for those who sent us. What do you say about yourself?" He said, "I am the voice of one crying in the wilderness, 'Make straight the way of the Lord,' as the prophet Isaiah said." (Jn 1:19-23)

And to his disciples, who were to become the disciples of Jesus, John explains further.

> You yourselves bear me witness, that I said, I am not the Christ, but I have been sent before him. He who has the bride is the bridegroom; the friend of the bridegroom, who stands and hears him, rejoices greatly at the bridegroom's voice; therefore this joy of mine is now full. He must increase, but I must decrease." (Jn 3:28-30)

Jesus is the divine bridegroom. The Church is his bride. And John the Baptist is the best man at the marriage, the "friend" who rejoices in the bridegroom's joy. His whole life and service was for the sake of Christ, whose way he prepared. He was faithful to Him unto his death, though even then he did not receive the answer which would have robbed him of the glory of his free and voluntary witness to the Truth for which he was born and for which he died.

Now when John in prison heard about the deeds of the Christ, he sent word by his disciples and said to him, "Are you he who is to come, or shall we look for another?" And Jesus answered them, "Go and tell John what you see and hear: the blind receive their sight and the lame walk, lepers are cleansed and the deaf hear, and the dead are raised up, and the poor have good news preached to them. And blessed is he who takes no offense (lit. *is not scandalized*) at me. As they went away, Jesus began to speak to the crowds concerning John: "What did you go out into the wilderness to behold? A reed shakend by the wind? Why then did you go out? To see a man clothed in soft raiment? Behold, those who wear soft raiment are in kings' houses. Why then did you go out? To see a prophet? Yes, I tell you, and more than a prophet. This is he of whom it is written, 'Behold, I send my messenger before thy face, who shall prepare thy way before thee.' Truly, I say to you, among those born of women there has risen no one greater than John the Baptist; yet he who is least in the kingdom of heaven is greater than he. From the days of John the Baptist until now the kingdom of heaven has suffered violence, and men of violence take it by force. For all the prophets and the law prophesied until John; and if you are willing to accept it, he is Elijah who is to come. He who has ears to hear, let him hear." (Mt 11:2-15)

It is not clear what Jesus meant when He said that "the least in the kingdom of heaven" is greater than John. Perhaps he spoke about Himself. Or perhaps he spoke about the Virgin Mary, and those Christians with her who by the grace of God lived to see the resurrection of Christ and to enter already baptized into His kingdom—unlike John who was beheaded before the Lord was crucified so that, as the Church teaches, he might be the Savior's forerunner even into death. But whatever it means, one thing remains clear. The Lord said that "among those born of women there has risen none greater than John the Baptist." And in Saint Luke's gospel, "I tell you, among those born of women none is greater than John." (Lk 7:28)

John the Baptist is the greatest. The reason is his violent dedication to Jesus which was the expression of his violent dedication to God's truth and justice. John's sheer, uncompromising righteousness is the cause of his greatness. There is nothing else. He was not one of the apostles. He did not witness the resurrection. He did not work miracles while he was alive. He did not write a book. He was not what one would call a mystic. But he was an ascetic and a prophet. He lived for God alone. And he bore witness to the Lord's commandments to his very last breath. The Church praises him for this, and especially glorifies him not only in his conception, nativity and beheading, but also on the festival held in his honor on the day after his baptism of the Lord.

> The memory of the righteous is with praise,
> And the witness to the Lord was sufficient for you,
>   O Forerunner.
> You were indeed revealed as the most honorable of the
>   prophets,
> For in the waters you baptized the One whom
>   you preached.
> And after suffering with joy for the sake of the Truth,
> You announced the glad tidings to those who were dead,
> Of the God who appeared in the flesh,
> Who takes away the sins of the world
> And grants us great mercy.[1]

[1]Troparion of the feast of the Synaxis of John the Baptist.

The Master proclaimed you to be a prophet,
Higher than all the prophets
And greater than any born of woman.
For the One whom all the prophets and the Law foretold,
You have beheld in the flesh.
Thus is truly the Christ.
And being more honored than all,
You have baptized Him.[2]

You came forth, O Baptist,
As a messenger from a barren womb.
And from your swaddling clothes you went to dwell
    in the wilderness.
You were the seal of all the prophets.
For you were made worthy to baptize in the Jordan
The One whom they had foretold in dark sayings
    and forms.
You heard the Father's voice from heaven testifying
    to His Son,
And you saw the Spirit in the form of a dove
Descending with the Father's words on the baptized One.
O Higher than all the prophets,
Do not cease to intercede for us
Who celebrate your memorial in faith![3]

[2]Hymn of Light of the feast of the Synaxis of John the Baptist.
[3]Matinal Hymn of the feast of the Synaxis of John the Baptist.

37

The Three Holy Hierarchs

The days following the feast of the Epiphany are filled with liturgical commemorations of great saints of the Church. We find during this time of year celebrations in honor of such men as Ignatius of Antioch, Gregory of Nyssa, Gregory the Theologian, John Chrysostom, Maximus the Confessor, Athanasius and Cyril of Alexandria and Mark of Ephesus; as well as the monastic saints Anthony, Paul, Macarius of Egypt, Euthymius, Theodosius and Ephraim of Syria. The month of January also includes the memory of such women martyrs as Domnica, Tatiana and Xenia. As such it is one of the richest times of the year for the contemplation of Christian sanctity.

On the thirtieth of the month, almost as a summary of the season, the Church celebrates the feast of the three holy hierarchs: Basil the Great, Archbishop of Caesarea in Cappadocia; Gregory the Theologian, bishop of Nazianzus and archbishop of Constantinople; and John Chrysostom of Antioch, also archbishop of Constantinople. This day is known in the Orthodox Church as the celebration of Orthodox letters, the feast of theological studies and ecclesiastical schools.

Let us who love their words come together with hymns,
To honor the three great torch-bearers of the Triune
    Godhead,
Basil the Great, Gregory the Theologian and
    John Chrysostom.
These men have enlightened the world with the rays
    of their divine doctrines.
They are flowing rivers of wisdom,

Who have filled all creation with springs of
    heavenly knowledge.
They ceaselessly intercede for us before the Holy Trinity.[1]

The three holy hierarchs were very different types of
people. Basil the Great (d. 379) was a diligent churchman, a
solid thinker, a compassionate pastor, a staunch defender of
orthodoxy and a monastic leader. Gregory the Theologian
(d. 389) was his best friend. They met together at the uni-
versity of Athens where they studied literature, rhetoric and
philosophy, only to abandon everything for the sake of following Christ. After spending time together in monastic solitude,
Basil took up the task of defending the divinity of Christ as
defined by the council of Nicea. He became a bishop and
forced his reluctant friend also to enter the episcopate and to
fight for the orthodox faith.

Gregory was a delicate man, a contemplative and a poet.
He was easily offended and often insulted. As a pastor he was
less than a success. But as a theologian, he was the greatest.
His homilies on the Holy Trinity, delivered to a tiny group
of faithful orthodox Christians in Constantinople when the
cathedral and the masses of the people were in the hands of
the Arian heretics, remain classics of Orthodox theology.

John Chrysostom (d. 407) was fiery preacher. He is called
Chrysostom, which means "golden-tongued," because of his
remarkable oratorical gifts. Saint John was solidly orthodox in
all of his teachings, but is not considered primarily as a theologian. He is remembered and praised more for his teachings
on the Christian life, his prophetic denunciations of injustice
and evil, his pastoral care for the poor and oppressed, and his
fearless opposition to those who would distort and betray the
gospel of Christ, especially those in high places of power and
responsibility. He died in exile, expelled from his church, in
407.

The three holy hierarchs were surrounded by small groups
of faithful supporters, including members of their families,
who assisted and inspired them in their work. Basil's mother

[1]Troparion of the feast of the Three Holy Hierarchs.

and grandmother, Emmelia and Macrina, as well as his sister Marcrina, are canonized saints of the Church, together with his brother Gregory of Nyssa. Both he and his brother Gregory considered their sister Macrina as their greatest teacher. Gregory the Theologian's mother Nonna is also a canonized saint. In his funeral oration for her, the holy father said that his mother gave him everything that he had in the Lord, including not only his physical life, but his spiritual life as well. Gregory's sister Theosebia, who some think was Gregory of Nyssa's wife, was praised by her brother as "greater than the priests," together with her sister Gorgonia. John Chrysostom's mother Anthusa is also a canonized saint of the church. His best friend and co-worker was the deaconess Olympiada (or Olympia), to whom he addressed his most moving letters at the end of his life. Thus we see that these great bishops, theologians and preachers were not alone in their efforts. They were in a real sense the products of a community of faith, devotion and learning; as well as its leaders and teachers.

In contemplating the lives and works of Basil, Gregory and John we realize, more than anything else, how a small group of faithful people can do much for the edification of the Church and the salvation of souls. We see also how no one can live in isolation, how even the greatest of the saints needed other saints to inspire and encourage them, to instruct and support them in their service. We see as well that intelligence and learning are not enough. Peoples' minds must be devoted to God and to divine wisdom and truth, but one must love God not only with all one's mind, but with all one's heart, soul and strength as well. The three holy hierarchs were men of ascetic discipline and fervent prayer. They were men of the Church, and not of the academy. And they were men who were willing not only to preach, but to practice what they preached; not only to talk but to work; and not only to work but to suffer for the Word of God Who came himself into the world not only to preach, but to suffer and die for the sake of the salvation of all.

The times in which the three hierarchs lived were terrible times for the Church, certainly not less dark and depressing than the present times, and perhaps even more so in many respects. But these men, and the women who stood with them, were able to persevere faithfully to the end. It is because of these people in the past that we have Christian life in the Church today.

Let us worthily honor the preachers of grace,
The resounding trumpets of the Spirit of God,
The mighty thunders roaring with the awesome Gospel,
Proclaiming the glory of God to the ends of the earth:
Basil the Great, Gregory the Theologian and
    John Chrysostom,
The three bright stars of the Holy Trinity.

Let us honor the champions of the Trinity,
The teachers of true worship,
The three apostles who walked in the spirit of the Twleve,
The rivers of Eden overflowing with living water,
Renewing the face of the earth with streams of theology,
Guiding the world to a new birth of faith.

Let us sound the trumpet with joy.
Let us celebrate the feast of our teachers with
    gladness and song.
Let us praise the three rivers of doctrine who
    revive our weary hearts.
They faithfully proclaimed the mysteries of the
    Holy Trinity.
Bless the wise hierarchs, all you who love wisdom.
Let the priests magnify these three great pastors.
They bring riches for the poor in spirit,
They intercede for the sinners,
The comfort the afflicted and guard those who travel,
Let us cry out to them, for they are quick to hear
    our desperate entreaties:
O Holy Teachers, save us from an evil generation
    and from eternal death.[2]

---

[2]Vespers of the feast of the Three Holy Hierarchs.

38

The Meeting of the Lord in the Temple

The Christmas-Epiphany season comes to an end with the feast of the Meeting of the Lord in the Temple on the second of February, forty days after the feast of the Savior's birth. Like most major festivals of the Church, the feast of the Lord's Meeting is kept with an eight-day postfeast celebration. The conclusion of this festival brings to a close the liturgical cycle which began at the beginning of the Christmas fast.

According to the Gospel of Saint Luke, Jesus was brought to the temple on the fortieth day after His birth in obedience to the Mosaic law which He as the Messiah had come to fulfill.

> And when the time came for their purification according to the law of Moses, they brought him up to Jerusalem to present him to the Lord (as it is written in the law of the Lord, "Every male that opens the womb shall be called holy to the Lord") and to offer a sacrifice according to what is said in the law of the Lord, "a pair of turtledoves, or two young pigeons."

The liturgy of the Church is clear about why this act of submission to the law of Moses was performed. We have already seen it in the act of Jesus' circumcision. The Lord had to do all things according to God's law so that in Him the law might be literally fulfilled in all of its details, and that this fulfillment might be given to all who accept Him.

> Today He who once gave the law to Moses on Sinai
> Submits Himself to the ordinances of the law,

For our sake becoming as we are, in His compassion.
Now the God of purity as a holy Child has opened
    a pure womb,
And as God is brought as an offering to Himself,
Setting us free from the curse of the law,
And granting light to our souls.[1]

When the Lord Jesus is brought by His parents to the temple, He is met there by the old man Simeon and the old woman Anna. It is from this meeting in the temple that the festival gets its name in the Orthodox Church.[2] This meeting is spiritually and theologically significant. It tells us that the Old is over and that the New has come. It tells us that the two covenants have now met: Israel has accomplished its God-given task in producing the Messiah. The promises made to Abraham in the beginning of the nation's calling have now been fulfilled. Israel's glory has dawned in the person of Christ who is now encountered in the world as the "light of revelation to the Gentiles." In Him the whole world is illumined and saved. The New Testament has come. God's final covenant community is established on earth. In Abraham's seed all the families of the world have been blessed. The old man and the old woman who meet Jesus in the temple and recognize Him for who He is symbolize in their oldness the passing away of the ancient customs, rituals and laws which were "but a shadow of the good things to come instead of the true form of these realities." (Heb 10:1) For, as the apostle Paul has said in another place, the ancient laws were "only a shadow of what is to come, but the substance belongs to Christ" who has brought to the whole world a "new creation." (Col 2:17, 1 Cor 5:17, Gal 6:15)

> Now there was a man in Jerusalem, whose name was Simeon, and this man was righteous and devout, look-ing for the consolation of Israel, and the Holy Spirit was upon him. And it had been revealed to him by the Holy Spirit that he should not see death before he had

[1]Vespers of the feast of the Meeting of the Lord in the Temple.
[2]In the Christian west this feast is called the Purification of Mary.

seen the Lord's Christ. And inspired by the Spirit he
came into the temple, and when the parents brought
in the child Jesus, to do for him according to the custom
of the law, he took him up in his arms and blessed
God and said, "Lord, now lettest thou thy servant
depart in peace, according to thy word; for mine eyes
have seen thy salvation which thou hast prepared in
the presence of all peoples, a light for revelation to
the Gentiles, and for glory to thy people Israel."

(. . .) And there was a prophetess Anna, the
daughter of Phanuel of the tribe of Asher; she was of
a great age having lived with her husband seven years
from her virginity, and as a widow till she was eighty-
four. She did not depart from the temple, worshipping
with fasting and prayer night and day. And coming
up at that very hour she gave thanks to God, and spoke
of him to all who were looking for the redemption
of Jerusalem. (Lk 2:25-38)

The old testament readings for the feast of the Meeting
tell how the children born to the people of Israel, male and
female, were to be offered in the temple, with sacrifices and
prayers. They also tell how the prophet Isaiah saw the Lord
in a vision, enthroned in the Jerusalem temple, and prophesied
that this same Lord would be worshipped by none other than
the Egyptians, the very symbol of the hostile Gentiles who
violently opposed the people of Israel and their God.[3]

In that day there will be an altar to the Lord in the
midst of the land of Egypt, and a pillar to the Lord at
its borders. It will be a sign and a witness to the Lord
of hosts in the land of Egypt; when they cry to the
Lord because of oppressors he will send them a savior,
and will defend and deliver them. And the Lord will
make himself known to the Egyptians and the Egyptians will know the Lord in that day and worship . . .

[3]The old testamental readings for the feast are a combination reading
from Exodus, Leviticus and Numbers; and two readings from Isaiah from
chapters 6 and 19.

and they will make vows to the Lord and perform them. (Isaiah 19:19-21)

Not only Egypt, but the whole world has received a Savior in the person of the Lord's Messiah; the Messiah who is Himself the Lord in human flesh. This is the astounding proclamation of the Meeting of the Lord in the temple. It is the reason for the great celebration which concludes the Winter Pascha.

He who is borne on high by the cherubim,
And praised in hymns by the seraphim,
Is brought today to the temple according to the law.
He rests on the arms of the old man as on a throne.
He receives from Joseph gifts befitting God:
A pair of doves which symbolize the spotless Church
And the newly-chosen people from among the Gentiles,
And two young pigeons, for He Who is presented is the
     originator of the two covenants, both old and new.
Simeon has now been granted the fulfillment of the
     prophecies concerning himself,
And he blesses Mary, the Virgin and Theotokos,
Foretelling in figures the passion of her Son.
From Him he begs release from this life, crying aloud:
Now let me depart in peace, O Master,
As You have promised me,
For I have seen the pre-eternal Light![4]

Rejoice, O Virgin Theotokos, full of grace!
From you shone the Sun of Righteousness, Christ our God!
Enlightening those who sat in darkness.
Rejoice, and be glad, O righteous Elder,
You accepted in your arms the Redeemer of our souls,
Who grants us the resurrection![5]

[4]Vespers of the feast of the Meeting of the Lord in the Temple.
[5]Troparion of the feast of the Meeting of the Lord in the Temple.

39

The Purification of Mary

In the Christian West the festival of the Meeting of the Lord in the Temple is called the feast of the Purification of the Blessed Virgin Mary. The accent of the celebration falls not so much on the encounter between the Christ Child and the old people who meet Him, but rather on the fact that the Mother of Jesus comes to be purified. This aspect of the evangelical story is not wholly absent from the liturgy of the Orthodox Church, but it is surely seen to be of secondary significance. The biblical law concerning the purification of the mother after childbirth is read at the service, but no mention is made of it in the hymns which stress the purity of the Virgin.

> For thus says the Lord God Almighty . . . it shall be that a woman who bears a male child, on the eighth day shall circumcise the flesh of the foreskin. Then for thirty-three days she shall not enter into the house of the Lord to the priest until the days of her purification are fulfilled . . . And after this she shall bring to the Lord an unblemished lamb one year old . . . and if she cannot afford a lamb, then she shall bring two turtle doves or two young pigeons, one for a burnt offering and the other for a sin offering; and the priest shall make atonement for her, and she shall be clean. (Lev 12)

We learn from the Church's liturgy that Joseph and Mary were considered to be poor, since they did not offer a lamb, but rather the turtle doves, as is depicted on the icons of the feast. The Gospel of Saint Luke makes no mention of the possibility of offering a lamb. We learn as well that, although the accent of the liturgy is on the meeting, Mary did in fact come for purification as the law required. This means that her womb was opened and that the Christ Child was born from her in the manner in which all children are born. In this sense, although the Church insists that Mary remains forever a virgin, the only miracle in regard to the Lord's birth is the virginal conception. There is no teaching of any other sort of miracle in regard to His birth; certainly no idea that He came forth from His mother without opening her womb.

But the question yet remains: What does it mean that Mary came for "purification?" It obviously cannot mean that there was any sin connected to her conceiving the Lord and giving Him birth as a man. This is especially so if it is automatically concluded, so to speak, that the act of sexual reproduction is always in some way a sin, since in Mary's case the teaching of the Gospel and the Church tradition is clear. Mary had no act of sexual union. Her conception is without knowing a man. The Lord begins to grow in her by the power of the Holy Spirit. So what can be the meaning of her "purification?"

The answer to this question, which pertains also to the Church's custom of "churching women" on the fortieth day after childbirth, undoubtedly has to do with the biblical understanding of "purification."[1] The scriptures teach that all people are sinful simply by being members of the human race. This does not mean that all people are personally guilty for "Adam's sin," which Orthodox doctrine categorically denies. Nor does it mean that every person necessarily and

---

[1]The Orthodox Church presently practices the rite of the churching of women after childbirth. This rite is usually performed on the fortieth day after the baby is born, or at the time when the woman resumes her normal activities, particularly attending church services and participating in Holy Communion. While the prayers of churching stress the sinfulness of the mother and ask for her forgiveness and purification, these petitions should never be understood to refer to the act of giving birth, and still less to the act by which children are conceived. St. John Chrysostom teaches that those who claim that the sexual act of reproduction is sinful are accusing God of sin, since He is the author of the act. St. John points out that the sexual act is sinful only when it is used wrongly, devoid of love and fidelity within the community of marriage. See John Chrysostom, *On Titus*, Homily 2.

inevitably sins in a personal manner, deliberately and consciously; which the Church tradition surely denies in the case of the Virgin Mary. It means rather that the entire human race, as an organic community of persons, is "missing the mark" (to *sin* literally mean to *miss the mark*) of its calling.

Humanity as a whole is off the track, it is not moving toward its created goal, which is perfection of life in communion with God. It is mortal, misdirected, fragmented and fallen apart. It is, in modern terms, alienated from its true being and estranged from its true purpose. And the Virgin Mary, like all mere human beings, is caught up in this fallenness and mortality by the mere fact of her being simply human.

In addition, the scriptures teach that all human beings, who are inevitably caught up in the falleness of the sinful world, are in need of "purification" when they come into direct contact with God, and especially when they are the objects of a direct divine action. God is always acting in our lives. But there are times when He acts directly, so to speak, and with particular purpose. These are the times of birth and death (and the times when we are in contact with those parts of our being which involve life and death, such as blood, menses and semen.) These are also times of worship, such as when the priests go into the Holy Place or when they touch the Holy Objects. Thus, according to the Mosaic law, mere human beings who were in direct touch with God through His concrete divine actions were required to offer signs of ritual "purification" to express the fact that being mere mortals and victims of sins (not to say sinners in their own right in virtually all cases) they had also been the objects of the holy actions of the Most High and Holy God.

If this is the proper understanding of the biblical teaching and practice of ritual "purification," and it seems that it is, then it becomes clear why the Blessed Virgin Mary, of all people, came to be "purified," and why all who follow in her example will do so as well. She came not because she had done anything sinful or wrong; certainly not in relation to her giving birth to the Savior. She came rather to show that she, being a mere mortal and in need of salvation along with the whole of creation, had been chosen to be the most active participant in the holiest act of God every accomplished in the world: the incarnation as a man of God's very own Son! To be required to participate in such a "purification" is the act of greatest joy and thanksgiving. It is also an act which brings the greatest glory and honor to the one who is "purified."

O Virgin Theotokos, Hope of all Christians!
Protect, preserve and save those who hope in You.

We the faithful saw the figure in the shadow of the law
    and in the scriptures.
Every male child that opened the womb was Holy to God.
Therefore we honor the first-born Son of the
    Unbegotten Father,
The first-born Son of the Unwedded Mother,

O Virgin Theotokos, Good Help of the world!
Protect and guard us from all necessity and sorrow.

The people of old offered a pair of doves and two
    young pigeons.
In their place the godly Elder and the sober-spirited
    Prophetess,
Ministered and gave glory to the Virgin's Child,
The only-begotten Son of the Father,
As He is brought into the temple of God.

O Pure Virgin Mother! That which was fulfilled in You
Is beyond the understanding of angels and mortal men.

You have committed to me the exceeding great joy
    of Your salvation, O Christ!
Simeon cried: Take Your servant who is weary
    of the shadow,
And make him a new preacher of the mystery of grace,
As he magnifies You in praise!

The Pure Dove, the Mother Lamb without blemish,
Brings the Shepherd and Lamb into the temple of God.

Holy Anna, sober in spirit and venerable in years,
Reverently confessed the Master freely and openly
    in the temple,
And she proclaimed Mary the Theotokos,
Magnifying her in the presence of all.

O Maiden Mary! Enlighten my soul
Which is grievously darkened by the passions of this life.[2]

---

[2]Ninth ode of the canon at matins, sung also as the Theotokos Hymn at the divine liturgy of the feast of the Meeting of the Lord in the Temple.

40

Mine Eyes Have Seen Thy Salvation

When the elder Simeon held the Christ Child in his arms at their meeting in the temple on the fortieth day after Jesus' birth, he said that he was now ready to die. He could depart in peace because his eyes had seen the Lord's Christ, the salvation which God had prepared from the foundation of the world which was now revealed in the presence of all people. According to St. Luke's Gospel, Simeon sang a song when he held the Christ Child in his arms and blessed God His Father. This canticle has become part of the Orthodox liturgy, being sung every evening at Vespers.

> Lord, now lettest Thou Thy servant depart in peace,
> According to Thy word,
> For mine eyes have seen Thy salvation
> Which Thou hast prepared before the face of all people,
> A light to enlighten the Gentiles,
> And the glory of Thy people, Israel.[1]

These words of the elder Simeon are placed on the lips of all Christians at the end of each day, which is the beginning of each liturgical day (for the Bible says that "there was evening and there was morning, one day," Gen 1:5), because all who have met the Lord are ready to die, for their eyes have beheld the salvation of the world.

The elder Simeon was inspired by the Holy Spirit to go to meet the Child Jesus in the temple. He was inspired by the

[1]See Lk 2:29-32. The translation here is that normally used at Orthodox liturgical services.

Spirit to know that he would not die before he had seen Him. He was inspired to recognize Him at His coming. He was inspired to proclaim Him as the Messiah who was "set for the fall and rising of many in Israel, and for a sign that is spoken against . . . that the thoughts of many hearts may be revealed." (Lk 2:34-35) And he was inspired to predict the sufferings which His mother Mary would endure when He would be nailed to the Cross, offering His life for the life of the world. For such is the traditional interpretation of his words concerning the sword that was to pierce Mary's soul. (See Lk 2:35)

Simeon was inspired by God's Spirit to meet Jeus Christ; to see and to bear witness. Surely he saw things that others never would see, and in fact did not see, in the same situation. For he was "righteous and devout, looking for the consolation of Israel, and the Holy Spirit was upon him." (Lk 2:25) Yet what Simeon saw, inspired though he was, is much less—at least humanly speaking—than what many others have seen. It is certainly less than what we ourselves have seen who live in the twentieth century of the Christian era.

We who live in the Church of Christ today have seen the Child Jesus. But we have also seen the grown-up Christ. We have seen the Lord not only as a little Child of forty days. But we have learned of the annunciation of the angel to the Virgin. We have been given insight into the miraculous manner of his birth. We have observed His circumcision on the eighth day, and His meeting in the temple with Simeon and Anna on the fortieth. We have stood at the Jordan and witnessed His encounter with the Baptist. We have listened to the testimony of the Forerunner, the friend of the Bridegroom who was sent to prepare His way. We have been present at the baptism, the Epiphany in the Jordan. We have heard the Father's voice and seen the Spirit descending and remaining upon Him, anointing Him in His humanity to be the Lord's Christ, the Messiah of God who is the Lord Himself as God's beloved Son. We have followed Him into the desert to be tempted by the devil. We have seen His words and observed His miracles. We have been confronted with His question: Who do you say that I am? And we have answered with

Peter and all of the apostles: You are the Christ, the Son of the living God! And we have gone with Him up to Jerusalem. We have eaten with Him in the upper room, enjoying the Master's hospitality, with uplifted minds. We have stood by the Cross. We have gone to the tomb. We have seen Him raised and glorified. We have been breathed upon and have received His Spirit. The tongues of fire which He came to cast upon the earth have been sent upon us. We have been anointed with His Spirit, filled with power from on high—the very same Spirit that inspired the elder Simeon to know that he would not die before he had seen the Savior, the Spirit that led him that day to the temple and moved him to sing the song that we all now sing each evening of our lives: For mine eyes have seen Thy salvation!

Our eyes have indeed seen God's salvation. For we have seen Christ. And even more. We have seen those who have seen Christ. We have seen Simeon and Anna, and with them, Mary the Virgin and Joseph. We have seen the Forerunner John, with all of the apostles. We have seen their successors, as well as their predecessors. We have seen the three young men in the fiery furnace of Babylon, and have beheld them singing and dancing in the flames. We have seen and heard the great assembly of forefathers and mothers, and have celebrated their memory with delight. We have observed the patriarchs and prophets who have told us of Christ's coming. And when He appeared, we have seen those who met Him and those who received Him. Following the apostles, we have observed the confessors and martyrs, and have sung praises to their blood as the seed of the Church. We have glorified the new covenant saints, the fathers and mothers: Basil, Gregory, John, Macrina, Nonna, Anthusa . . . and the numberless holy people who have seen and loved the Lord down through the ages, just unto our own, to our beloved Saint Herman of Alaska, and our beloved Father Alexander.

Humanly speaking we have seen much more than Simeon saw that day in the temple; incomparably more! Yet it may sadly have to be said that with the eyes of our spirits we have seen incomparably less. If this is so, it is no fault of the Lord's. For He has done everything that we might see

Him in the Spirit in the midst of His Church. He has done everything that the words of the letter of Peter in the scriptures could be applied directly to us:

> Blessed be the God and Father of our Lord Jesus Christ! By his great mercy we have been born anew to a living hope through the resurrection of Jesus Christ from the dead, and to an inheritance which is imperishable, undefiled and unfading, kept in heaven for you, who by God's power are guarded through faith for a salvation ready to be revealed in the last time. In this you rejoice, though now for a little while you may have to suffer various trials, so that the genuineness of your faith, more precious than gold which though perishable is tested by fire, may redound to praise and glory and honor at the revelation of Jesus Christ. Without having seen him you love him; though you do not now see him, you believe in him and rejoice in him with unutterable and exalted joy. As the outcome of your faith you obtain the salvation of your souls. (1 Pet 1:3-9)

We have not seen Jesus with our human eyes; and we do not now see Him. But we believe in Him and love Him and rejoice in Him with unutterable and exalted joy. We behold Him with the eyes of our spirits when, inspired by His Spirit, we celebrate in the Church each year the Winter Pascha of His Coming.

> The Lover of Man,
> Who fulfills everything in the law,
> Is now brought into the temple of God.
> Simeon the elder receives Him in his aged arms crying:
> Let me now depart to the blessed life,
> For today I see You clothed in mortal flesh,
> The Lord of life and the Master of death.
>
> You have shone forth, O Lord,
> O Light of revelation to the Gentiles.

You are the Sun of Righteousness,
Enthroned upon a radiant cloud.
You have fulfilled the shadows of the law.
The grace of renewal begins to shine.
When Simeon received You he cried out in joy:
Release me now from corruption,
For today I have seen You, my Master!

Today the holy Mother who is beyond all temples,
Enters into the temple of God.
She reveals to the world its Creator,
And the Giver of the law.
Simeon the elder receives Him in his arms.
He worships Him and cries out:
Lord now let Your servant depart in peace,
For I have seen You—the Savior of our souls![2]

[2]Vespers of the last day of the postfeast of the Meeting of the Lord in the Temple.